GCSE
Geography
for WJEC A

Andy Owen, Jo Pritchard,
Colin Lancaster, Jacqui Owen
& Dirk Sykes

CORE

HODDER
EDUCATION
AN HACHETTE UK COMPANY

Acknowledgements

Text extracts and screenshots

p.14 *r* and **p.15** *bl* Plan of the Boscastle flood defences, the Environment Agency/NCDC; **p.16** 'Your flood plan' screenshot, the Environment Agency; **p.18** Screenshot from Future flooding report, p.103, www.foresight.gov.uk/ Flood%20and%20Coastal%20Defence/Chapter4a.pdf; **p.22** Screenshot of flood map from Environment Agency website; **p.31** *b* screenshot of frogspawn © The Woodland Trust; **p.33** Dr Malcolm Ramsay, © Jim Metzner Productions, Inc.; **p.38** Computer models from the Intergovernmental Panel on Climate Change (IPCC); **p.44** The Beddington Zero Energy Development (BedZed) from *www.eco-schools.org.uk;* **p.53** Screenshot showing geothermal zones and active volcanoes in south-west Iceland from *http://gullhver.os.is;* **p.57** Montserrat visitor statistics, 2002-2006 (Organisation of Eastern Caribbean States); **p.59** Monitoring activity at the Soufriere Hills Volcano by the Montserrat Volcano Observatory; **p.62** *l* Flyer for a 'Shake Out' event from *www.shakeout.org;* **p.65** Hazard alert table for Montserrat redrawn from *www.mvo.ms;* **p.67** *all* Screenshots from Worldmapper homepage, *www.worldmapper.org,* © 2006 SASI Group (University of Sheffield) and Mark Newman (University of Michigan); **p.75** *cr* Comparing occupations in Shrewsbury and Bishop's Castle from *2001 Census;* **p.79** *b* Screenshot from National Statistics website, *www.statistics.gov.uk/census2001/pyramids/ pages/uk.asp;* **p.86-87** *all* Screenshots showing world population maps and pyramids from *www.population.action.org;* **pp.91, 92** and **93** Global distribution of Nokia's factories, laboratories and offices; and sales and employees, 2003-7; **p.95** International Telecommunications Union, screenshot of mobile phone subscribers in Africa from *www.itu.int;* **p.98** Extract from *World Migration 2005: Costs and Benefits of International Migration* (IMO); **p.99** Screenshot source: Eurostat; **p.100** *tl* Location statistics of the world's biggest 2000 companies (Forbes, 2008); **p.104** *t* Screenshot map of Coca-Cola plants from http://www.coca-colaindia.com; **p.105** Extract on Coca-Cola from India Resource Centre website; **p.121** *all* Screenshots from interactive world map © The World Bank, *http://devdata.worldbank.org/atlas-mdg;* **p.124** Web extract from the Department for International Development (DFID). An updated article is available at *http://www.dfid.gov.uk/Global-Issues/ Millennium-Development-Goals/2-Achieve-Universal-primary-education;* **p.128** *b* Screenshot showing the proportion of population using improved (safe) drinking water, © Copyright United Nations Development Programme, *www.mdgmonitor.org.*

Crown copyright material is reproduced under Class Licence Number C02P0000060 with the permission of the Controller of HMSO.

Map on **p.12** reproduced from Ordnance Survey mapping with the permission of the Controller of HMSO, © Crown copyright. All rights reserved. Licence no. 100036470,

Although every effort has been made to ensure that website addresses are correct at time of going to press, Hodder Education cannot be held responsible for the content of any website mentioned in this book. It is sometimes possible to find a relocated web page by typing in the address of the home page for a website in the URL window of your browser.

Hachette UK's policy is to use papers that are natural, renewable and recyclable products and made from wood grown in sustainable forests. The logging and manufacturing processes are expected to conform to the environmental regulations of the country of origin.

Orders: please contact Bookpoint Ltd, 130 Milton Park, Abingdon, Oxon OX14 4SB. Telephone: (44) 01235 827720. Fax: (44) 01235 400454. Lines are open 9.00–5.00, Monday to Saturday, with a 24-hour message-answering service. Visit our website at www.hoddereducation.co.uk.

First published in 2009 by Hodder Education,
An Hachette UK company,
338 Euston Road,
London NW1 3BH

Impression number	5 4 3 2
Year	2012 2011 2010 2009

Cover photo: Volcano crater, New Hebrides, Australasia © Larry Dale Gordon/zefa/Corbis
Illustrations by Barking Dog Art, Oxford Designers & Illustrators and DC Graphic Design Ltd
Typeset in 10.5pt Trade Gothic by DC Graphic Design Ltd, Swanley Village, Kent
Printed in Italy

A catalogue record for this title is available from the British Library

ISBN: 978 0340 98374 4

Contents

GCSE Geography for WJEC Specification A is a new geography course designed for students in England and Wales. The topics that have been selected will help you to make sense of the rapidly changing world in which we live. This book examines current issues that have a life changing impact on millions of people: such as climate change, earthquake hazards, floods, health concerns, globalisation and poverty.

I was thrilled to be asked by WJEC to help structure this new course and I have really enjoyed writing this book. I hope that you will find it useful for your course and that it will inspire you to take a greater interest in a wider study of geography.

Andy Owen

The main features of the book

This book includes features that have been designed to help you make the most of your course and prepare you for your examinations. These are:

- GIS activities that explain how digital technology is used to store and retrieve geographical information.
- Advice from one of the examiners, who shows how to get the best mark from common exam questions.
- Sections in which you are asked to predict what might happen to geography in the future, in 20, 50 or 100 years.
- Case studies of real places to illustrate the concepts you have studied.

Geographical Information Systems (GIS)

A Geographical Information System (GIS) is a way of storing digital geographical data on a computer or server. Most GIS systems will allow the user to interact with the data to produce a custom-made table, graph or map. Some companies sell GIS programs that will allow you to collect, store and process data on your school's computer system. However, not every school has these programs, so the GIS panels in this book give you the web addresses of some useful GIS sites that are available free on the internet. These sites will allow you to view and process the data that they have collected, but in most cases you cannot add data of your own.

The ability to plan and conduct a geographical enquiry (or investigation) is an essential part of your GCSE. You can use these GIS sites to find geographical data that could help you in your own geographical enquiries.

Examiner's Tips

The examiner's advice panels are designed to help you prepare for standard questions that are asked in the examinations. They have been written by Dirk Sykes, principal examiner for WJEC, responsible for question setting and leading a team of examiners who mark the examinations.

Geographical Futures

An exciting recent development in geographical education has been the idea that we should be able to use our understanding of geographical processes and patterns to predict what might happen in the future. This is a particularly important aspect of your course so there are lots of pages in this book devoted to 'Geographical Futures'. It makes sense to plan for the future, so Geographical Futures pages address issues such as:

- How will climate change affect our lives?
- Is extreme weather getting more common and how can we best protect ourselves from river and coastal floods in the future?
- How and why are populations of countries changing and how can we best tackle diseases such as malaria?

Case studies

A case study is a detailed example of a geographical concept or issue. You will need to learn a few case studies so that you can show in the examinations that you know about real places. You will need to know:

- The name of the place and where in the world your case study is located.
- What the case study is a good example of.
- A few simple facts or figures about the case study.

The location of the case studies (that are outside the UK) are shown on this world map.

Figure 1 The location of case studies (outside the UK) that are used in this book

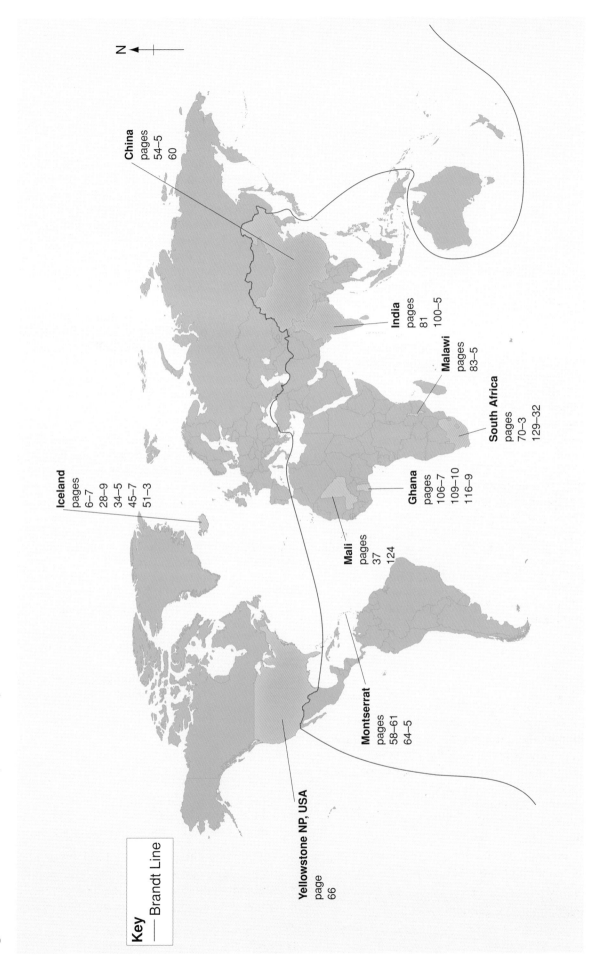

N

Key
— Brandt Line

China
pages
54–5
60

India
pages
81
100—5

Malawi
pages
83–5

South Africa
pages
70–3
129–32

Ghana
pages
106–7
109–10
116–9

Mali
pages
37
124

Iceland
pages
6–7
28–9
34–5
45–7
51–3

Yellowstone NP, USA
page
66

Montserrat
pages
58–61
64–5

Photo acknowledgements

The publishers would like to thank the following for permission to reproduce copyright material:

p.1 © Andy Owen; **p.2** © Andy Owen; **p.3** *all* © Andy Owen; **p.4** © Colin Lancaster; **p.5** *t* © Colin Lancaster, *b* © Andy Owen; **p.6** © Andy Owen; **p.7** © Andy Owen; **p.8** © PA Photos; **p.9** © Simon Robinson, 2004; **p.13** © Patryk Galka/iStockphoto.com; **p.14** © Andy Owen; **p.15** © *tl & tr* © Andy Owen; **p.17** © Steve Sant/Alamy; **p.18** *t* © Oliver Malms/iStockphoto.com; **p.19** © PA Photos/AP/Debra Gulbas; **p.20** © Oliver Malms/iStockphoto.com; **p.23** © Rex Features/James D. Morgan; **p.26** © Nick Cobbing/Alamy; **p.28** © Icelandic Photo Agency/Alamy; **p.29** © Patryk Galka/iStockphoto.com; **p.30** *tr* © Nature Picture Library/Mats Forsberg; **p.31** *tl & tr* © The Woodland Trust; **p.32** *l* © Skyscan/Corbis, *t* © Rex Features/Sipa Press, *br* © Corbis/Arko Data/Reuters; **p.34** *tl* © Oliver Malms/iStockphoto.com, *tr* © Getty Images/photographer's choice; **p.36** © Oliver Malms/iStockphoto.com; **p.37** © Getty Images/Daniel Pepper; **p.38** © Oliver Malms/iStockphoto.com; **p.39** © Eduardo Abad/epa/Corbis; **p.40** © Oliver Malms/iStockphoto.com; **p. 44** © Raf Makda/View Pictures/Rex Features; **p.45** © David Lyon/Alamy; **p.47** © Andy Owen; **p.49** © imagebroker/Alamy; **p.50** © R. Stewart, copyright © 2008 Monserrat Volcano Observatory; **p.51** © Throstur Thordarson/Nordic photos/Photolibrary; **p. 52** © Magnus T. Gudmundsson, University of Iceland; **p.53** © Sigurjón Sindrason; **p.54** *all* © LIU JIN/AFP/Getty Images; **p.55** © Sipa Press/Rex Features; **p.56** © Paul A. Souders/Corbis; **p.58** Reproduced with the permission of the British Geological Survey © NERC. All rights Reserved;

p.60 © Wang Xiwei/ChinaFotoPress/Getty Images; **p.63** *all* © R. Stewart and E. Joseph, copyright © 2009 Monserrat Volcano Observatory; **p.66** *tl* © Oliver Malms/iStockphoto.com; **p.66** *br* © C. Barry – Fotolia.com; **p. 68** © Stan Gamester/Alamy; **p.74** *l* © Getty Images/Maeers/Hulton, *r* Still Pictures/Paul Glendell; **p.85** © Panos Pictures/Alfredo Caliz; **p.88** © Oliver Malms/iStockphoto.com; **p.89** *tl* © Still Pictures/Ron Giling, *tr* © Getty Images/Raveendran/AFP, *bl* © PETER PARKS/AFP/Getty Images, *br* © Corbis/Strauss/Curtis; **p.90** © Nokia 2009, **p.92** © Corbis/Andreas Gebert/DPA; **p.93** © Corbis/Claro Cortes IV/Reuters; **p.97** © PA Photos/Kirsty Wigglesworth; **p. 100** © Stuart Freedman/Panos Pictures; **p.101** © Rex Features; **p.103** © Patryk Galka/iStockphoto.com; **p.104** © Getty Images/Raveendran/AFP; **p.106** © Corbis/Flip Schulke; **p.107** *l* © Christian Aid/Austin Hargreaves, *r* © Corbis/Reinhard Krause/Reuters, *br* © Panos Pictures/Karen Robinson; **p.109** © Christian Aid/Penny Tweedie; **p.110** *l* © Reproduced with kind permission of Oxfam, *r* © Greg Williams/Oxfam; **p.111** *l* © Panos Pictures/Christien Jaspars, *r* © *Thin Black Lines* (1988), p24; **p.113** © *Thin Black Lines* (1988); **p.117** © Panos Pictures/Karen Robinson; **p.118** © Still Pictures/Jorgen Schytte; **p.122** *all* © United Nations Development Programme; **p. 123** *t* © Panos Pictures/Giacomo Pirozzi; **p.123** *b* © Patryk Galka/iStockphoto.com; **p.124** © Panos Pictures/Crispin Hughes; **p.126** © United Nations Development Programme; **p.128** © United Nations Development Programme; **p.130** © Transformation Resource Centre; **p.132** *t* © International Water Management, *b* © PlayPumps International.

What are river processes and what landforms do they create?

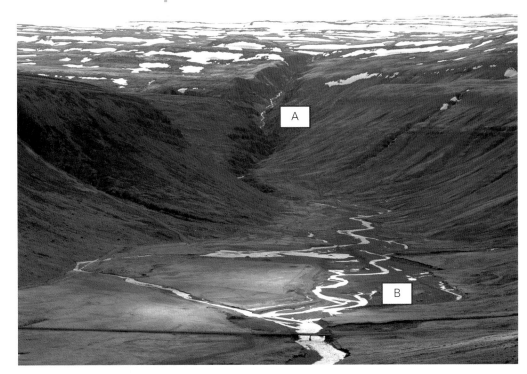

Figure 1 What landform processes created this landscape?

Activity

1. Work in pairs. Discuss the landscape in Figure 1 before answering the following questions.
   a) Describe how the river and its valley change as it flows towards you. Use the following table to compare the river and its valley at A and B.

	River at A	River at B
Gradient of channel (steepness of the river)		
Width of valley floor		
Shape of river channel (plan view)		
Words that describe the landforms you can see		
The processes that might occur in this section of river		

   b) How might climate affect the development of a landscape? Think particularly about the upland area across the top of the photo. Using evidence from this part of the photo explain how the climate might affect the river and the vegetation.

2. This photo was taken at 65° North and the mountains are 600 metres above sea level.
   The photo was taken in May.
   a) Suggest how this landscape would be different in winter.
   b) Suggest how this location could affect the river processes throughout the year.

River processes

Figure 2 A number of different river processes are evident in this Icelandic river

From the moment water begins to flow over the surface of the land, gravity gives it the power to erode the landscape. The gravitational energy of the flowing water enables the river to **transport** its **load** of boulders, gravel, sand and silt downstream. Where energy levels are high the main river process is **erosion**. At other times of the year, or in other parts of the river where energy levels are lower, the main process is **deposition**.

Erosion occurs where the river has plenty of energy so, for example, where the river is flowing quickly or when the river is full of water after heavy rain. Rivers that are flowing across gentle slopes (such as at B in Figure 1 or the river in Figure 2) tend to flow with greatest force on the outer bend of each curve (or **meander**). Water is thrown sideways into the river bank, which is eroded by both hydraulic action and abrasion. The bank gradually becomes undercut. The overhanging soil slumps into the river channel where this new load of material can be picked up and transported downstream by the flowing water.

Transportation process	Sediment size or type	Typical flow conditions	Description of the process
Solution	Soluble minerals such as calcium carbonate	Any	Minerals are dissolved from soil or rocks and carried along in the flow
Suspension	Small particles e.g. clay and silt	Suspension occurs in all but the slowest flowing rivers	Tiny particles are carried long distances in the flowing water
Saltation	Sand and small gravels	More energetic rivers with higher velocities	The sediment bounces and skips along
Traction	Larger gravels, cobbles and boulders	Only common in high energy river channels or during flood events	The bed load rolls along in contact with the river bed

Figure 3 The transportation of sediment

C

Erosional processes

Hydraulic action – water crashes into gaps in the soil and rock, compressing the air and forcing particles apart

Abrasion – the flowing water picks up rocks from the bed that smash against the river banks

Attrition – rocks carried by the river smash against one another, so they wear down into smaller and more rounded particles

Corrosion – minerals such as calcium carbonate (the main part of chalk and limestone rocks) are dissolved in the river water

Figure 4 Four processes of river channel erosion

The process of deposition occurs where the river loses its energy. For example, where a river enters a lake and its flow is slowed by the body of still water. Deposition also occurs in very shallow sections of a river channel where friction between the river bed and the water causes the river to lose its energy and deposit its load. The process of deposition creates layers of sand and gravel that are often sorted by sediment size because the coarsest sediment is deposited first.

Activity

1 Study Figure 2. Use evidence from the photograph to suggest what river processes are occurring at A, B and C.

2 Draw four diagrams or cartoons to illustrate the ways in which a river transports material.

3 Study Figure 5 and explain how erosion, transportation and deposition have created this landform.

4 Study Figures 1, 2 and 5. Use evidence in these photos to explain the difference between abrasion, hydraulic action and attrition.

Figure 5 This river channel has split into a number of smaller distributaries as it flows into this much larger body of water

3

Investigating river processes and landforms

The river at A in Figure 1 and the river in Figure 6 show typical features of a river flowing over steeper gradients. These rivers are eroding vertically more than from side to side. As the river erodes downwards it cuts into its channel and produces a narrow valley with steep V-shaped sides. The rocks of the river bed may show evidence of abrasion in the form of smoothly cut **potholes** (also known as scour holes).

Rivers flowing over steep gradients have enough energy to erode and transport a large quantity of material. The load on the river bed here is large and angular. As a river flows downstream the process of attrition gradually reduces the overall size of the load.

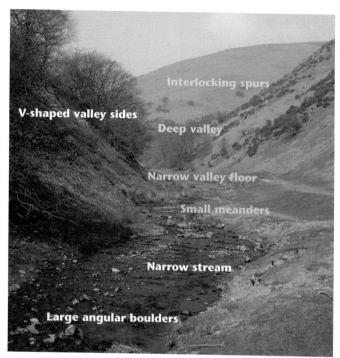

Figure 6 Ashes Valley, Shropshire is a typical **V-shaped valley**. The National Trust owns the site and encourages students to visit. As many as 40,000 geography students visit every year

Rivers flowing over gentle gradients tend to swing from side to side. The water flows fastest on the outside bend of each meander. This causes erosion of the banks rather than the bed, a process known as **lateral erosion**. Meanwhile, the slow flowing water on the inside of each bend loses energy and deposits its load. The material is sorted with the larger gravel being deposited first, then the sand and finally the silt.

Meandering rivers such as the River Severn shown in Figure 8 tend to flow across a wide **floodplain**. This feature has been created over many thousands of years by the processes of lateral erosion and deposition.

Figure 7 Sediment size (cm) from two sites in Ashes Valley, Shropshire

Site 1 Upstream			Site 2 Downstream		
Left bank	Middle	Right bank	Left bank	Middle	Right bank
16.1	22.0	10.1	7.8	11.1	2.4
10.4	10.5	10.4	7.6	2.1	6.1
22.0	9.0	3.0	3.6	7.0	1.8
6.5	3.6	1.5	1.5	1.3	10.6
12.0	7.9	6.4	1.4	2.7	6.0
7.4	2.1	6.0	2.2	5.1	2.0
7.4	3.5	1.6	9.0	1.1	6.7
6.5	8.9	3.8	0.9	1.3	2.1
11.0	8.4	5.4	4.3	2.0	4.7

Activity

1 Study Figure 6. Explain how each of the following features was formed:
   a) V-shaped valley sides
   b) large angular boulders in the stream bed
   c) interlocking spurs.

2 A student has collected sediment data from two sites in Ashes Valley and put it in a table (Figure 7).
   a) Draw a graph to compare the sediment size for the two sites.
   b) Describe how the size of the sediment changes:
      i) across the width of the river
      ii) as the river moves downstream.
   c) Explain the processes that cause the sediment size to change.

3 Study Figures 8 and 9. Describe each of the following features and explain how it was formed:
   a) point bar
   b) floodplain.

4 a) Use the information in Figures 10 and 11 to draw a cross section of the River Onny.
   b) Describe and explain the shape of this channel.

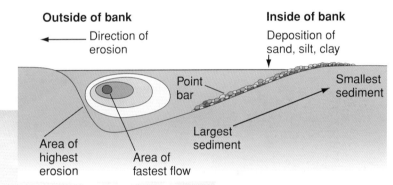

Figure 8 Features of river meanders and floodplain of the River Severn at Ironbridge

Figure 9 Processes at work on a river meander

Figure 10 Collecting data in order to draw a cross section of a river channel, the River Onny, Shropshire

Width across river (m)	0	0.5	1.0	1.5	2.0	2.5	3.0	3.5	4.0	4.5	5.0	5.5	6.0	6.5	7.0
Depth to bed from line (cm)	20	115	112	102	87	82	78	80	72	68	60	55	48	42	36

Figure 11 Depth measurements taken by students in the River Onny. The depth of water at 4 m across the stream was 22 cm

Iceland

Investigating river landforms: waterfalls and gorges

Iceland has a large number of waterfalls including Gullfoss and Dettifoss, which are Europe's largest waterfalls. In this case study we will investigate some of the different ways in which waterfalls are made.

Figure 12 Gullfoss waterfall. The upper step of the falls can be clearly seen in the upper part of the photo. The top of the second step can be seen at the bottom of the photo

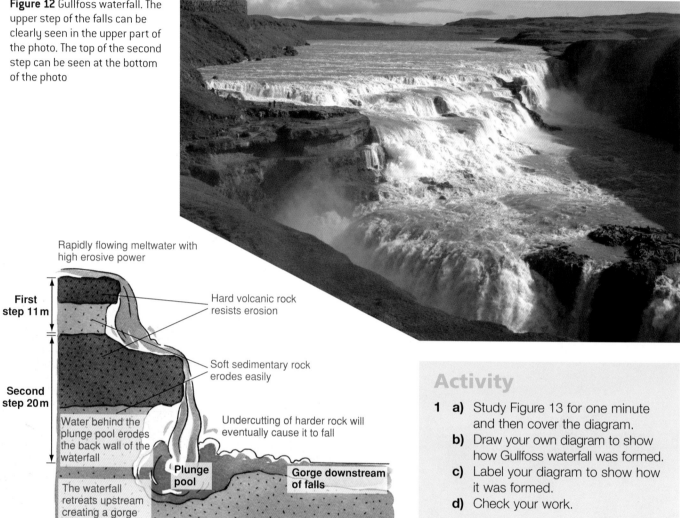

Rapidly flowing meltwater with high erosive power

First step 11 m

Hard volcanic rock resists erosion

Soft sedimentary rock erodes easily

Second step 20 m

Water behind the plunge pool erodes the back wall of the waterfall

Undercutting of harder rock will eventually cause it to fall

Plunge pool

Gorge downstream of falls

The waterfall retreats upstream creating a gorge

Figure 13 Features and processes that produce the waterfall at Gullfoss

Activity

1. **a)** Study Figure 13 for one minute and then cover the diagram.
   b) Draw your own diagram to show how Gullfoss waterfall was formed.
   c) Label your diagram to show how it was formed.
   d) Check your work.

Gullfoss waterfall is located in central southern Iceland, 100 km east of the capital city Reykjavik. It is where the River Hvitá drops a total of 31 m over two vertical steps. Below the waterfall is a narrow valley with almost vertical sides. This feature is known as a **gorge**. Gullfoss and its gorge were formed by the processes of river erosion. The landscape here is made of alternating layers of lava and sedimentary rocks. The lava is very resistant to erosion whereas the sedimentary rocks are eroded more easily. As the river plunges over the first thin layer of lava it pours on to the softer rock below. A combination of hydraulic action and abrasion erodes this rock relatively easily creating a plunge pool. Abrasion at the back of the plunge pool undercuts the layers of volcanic rock. Eventually this overhang will fracture and the rocks will fall into the plunge pool where they are broken up by attrition. So each step is gradually cut back and the waterfall retreats backwards along the river's course. It is this process of retreat that has cut the gorge.

How else are waterfalls formed?

Many waterfalls in Iceland (and in other parts of northern Europe including the UK) are formed due to landform processes that occurred at the end of the ice age around 10,000 years ago. During the ice age, ice sheets expanded over large parts of central Iceland and valley glaciers flowed from these ice sheets towards the sea. The glaciers carved deep, steep sided or **U-shaped valleys** into the landscape. Figure 14 shows how this glacial landscape created the waterfalls we see today.

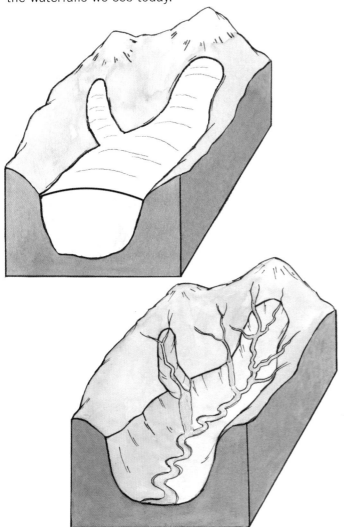

Figure 14 Glacial landscape and today's landscape

years before present		
12,000	glacial period	Huge amounts of water were trapped in ice sheets and glaciers. Sea levels were much lower than today.
10,000	gradually warming	As the ice melted the glaciers retreated and meltwater ran into the sea. Sea levels began to rise.
8,000		
6,000	warmest period	Sea levels reached a peak. Waves cut cliffs 40–60 metres high along the southern coastline.
4,000		The weight of ice during the glacial period had forced the crust to sink slightly. Now that the weight of ice had gone the crust began to slowly rise back up again. The effect of this is that the sea level slowly fell. The sea cliffs on the south coast were raised above sea level and the coastline retreated several kilometres creating new flat land along Iceland's south coast.
2,000		
today		

Figure 15 Timeline explaining the impact of the ice age on sea levels around Iceland

Figure 16 Seljalandsfoss waterfall, south Iceland, plunges over a raised sea cliff

Activity

2 Study the pair of diagrams in Figure 14. Use as many geographical terms as you can to explain how today's landscape has been formed.

3 Use Figure 15 to draw a series of simple diagrams or cartoons to show how the height of the sea level has changed. Use these diagrams to explain why there are so many waterfalls in south Iceland.

Why did this river flood?

What can be done to manage the river in the future?

Figure 17 The floods in Boscastle, Cornwall, in August 2004

How do river processes and landforms affect the lives of people?

The River Valency is a short river that flows in a steep V-shaped valley into the sea at Boscastle, Cornwall. Normally, the hills that form the catchment area for the River Valency get 100–120 mm of rainfall during August. But on the afternoon of 16 August 2004, the hills above Boscastle were hit by a freak rain storm. In just four hours 200 mm of rainfall fell causing the river to burst its banks. The river flooded the town's car park and carried 80 cars out into the sea. The force of the water rushing through the town caused the collapse of five buildings and another 37 were damaged. Thankfully nobody was killed during this flood. Emergency helicopters arrived quickly and were able to rescue people from the rooftops of flooded buildings.

During the flood of 2004 it is estimated that the River Valency had the same amount of water flowing in it as the River Thames where it flows past the Houses of Parliament in London. Every litre of water weighs one kilogram so you can imagine how much force the river had to perform hydraulic action. Rivers that are in flood are also able to transport much more load. During this flood the River Valency had enough energy to pick up and carry large boulders. This caused abrasion of the bed and banks. As flood water leaves the channel and flows over the floodplain it loses its energy and large quantities of sediment are deposited.

Movement of water through the drainage basin

To understand flood events like the one in Boscastle we need to understand the way in which the drainage basin of a river works. Very little precipitation falls directly into rivers. Most falls on hillsides, fields and forests and takes time to enter a river. Precipitation falling in the drainage basin shown in Figure 18 may take one of a number of different routes before it enters the river. On hitting the ground, surface water will either flow over the surface as **overland flow** or it will **infiltrate** into the soil store. Once in the soil, water moves slowly downhill as **throughflow**. Eventually soil water **percolates** deeper into the ground and enters the bedrock where it continues to travel as **groundwater flow**. Rates of infiltration, throughflow and groundwater flow will depend on the type of soil and rock.

Figure 18 Stores and flows of water in a natural drainage basin

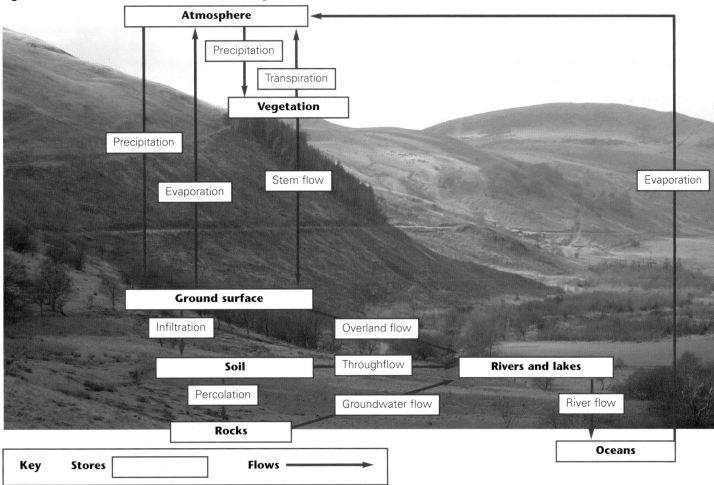

Activity

3 Use Figure 18 to name:
   a) three surface stores of water
   b) two places water is stored below the surface.

4 Suggest why precipitation falling into a drainage basin of impermeable rocks is likely to reach the river much more quickly than rainwater falling in an area of porous rocks.

5 Figure 18 and the text on this page contain many new terms. Make a list of at least 12 words that are used when describing water stores and flows in the drainage basin and write your own definitions for them.

Why do floods occur?

Flooding occurs when conditions cause water to flow overland rather than by infiltrating into the soil. A flood can occur when:

- the ground is already saturated with water after a long period of rain
- the ground is frozen
- the rainfall is so intense that all of it cannot soak into the ground.

Paving over the soil creates an impermeable surface, so the growth of urban areas increases the risk of flooding. A flood hydrograph shows the discharge of a river over the period of a flood. The example in

Figure 19 shows how a small river might respond to a flood event. The blue bar represents a sudden downpour of rain, like the one at Boscastle. In this example it takes two hours for overland flow from the drainage basin to reach the river channel. At this point the amount of water in the channel rises rapidly. The time between the peak rainfall and the **peak discharge** is known as **lag time**. The lag time and height of the peak discharge depend on the features of the drainage basin. In drainage basins where infiltration is reduced, the lag time will be shorter and the peak discharge larger. Some of these factors are illustrated in Figures 20 and 21.

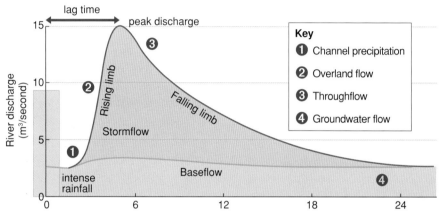

Figure 19 A simple flood hydrograph

Activity

1 Study Figure 19.
   a) Use times and discharge figures from the hydrograph to describe:
      i) the shape of the rising limb and the lag time
      ii) the shape of the falling limb and baseflow.
   b) Use your understanding of Figure 18 on page 9 to explain how overland flow, throughflow and groundwater flow all contribute to a flood at different times.

River Valency

Case study of the drainage basin of the River Valency

The River Valency in Cornwall is a very short river as it flows less than 10 km from its **source** to its **mouth**. The source of the river is at 280 metres above sea level. The high source and short length make the river's gradient rather steep. The total size of the drainage basin is around 26 km². The rocks of the drainage basin are mainly slates, which are **impermeable**. The river has a number of small tributaries. These streams have cut deep V-shaped valleys into this landscape.

There are no large towns in the drainage basin. Boscastle itself covers less than 1 km². The upland part of the drainage basin is used for grazing. Some of the valleys are wooded. Trees help to remove some water from the soil before it reaches the river. However, during flood events, tree branches that are overhanging the river can be broken off. These branches then restrict the flow of water in the river, especially if they get caught against the piers of bridges. In these conditions a narrow stone bridge begins to act more like a dam than a bridge causing the river channel to become blocked.

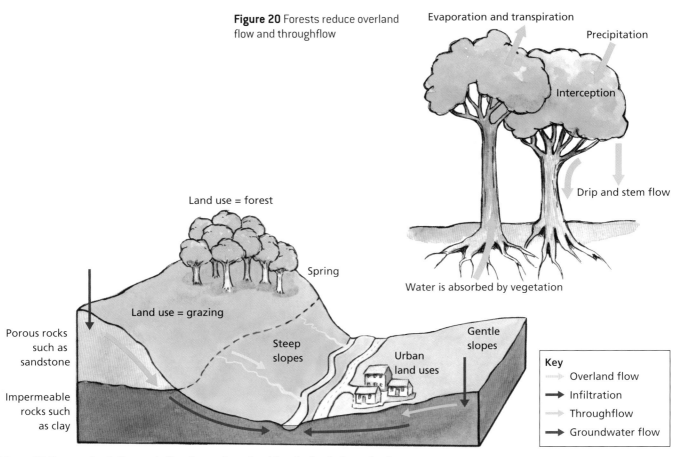

Figure 20 Forests reduce overland flow and throughflow

Figure 21 Factors that influence infiltration and overland flow in the drainage basin

Activity

2 Use Figure 20 to explain how cutting down a large forest could affect lag time and peak discharge in a nearby river.

3 Use Figures 18, 19, 20 and 21 to help you copy and complete the following table.

Drainage basin factor	Impact on infiltration	Impact on overland flow and throughflow	Impact on lag time
Steep slopes			
Gentle slopes			
Porous rocks			
Impermeable rocks			
Urban land uses			
Planting more trees			

4 Draw a pair of flood hydrographs to show the difference between similar sized drainage basins that have:
   a) porous rocks compared with impermeable rocks
   b) urban land uses compared with lots of forests.

5 Suggest how the features of the drainage basin of the River Valency affected the river's lag time during the 2004 flood.

River Valency drainage basin

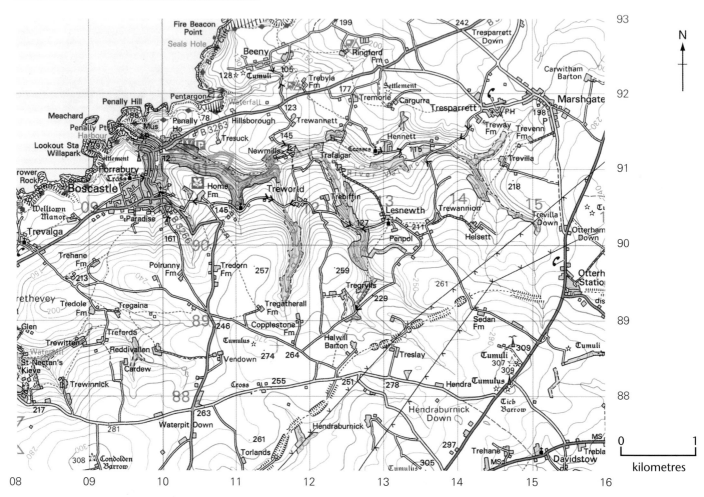

Figure 22 An Ordnance Survey extract of the catchment area of the River Valency. Scale 1:50,000 Sheet 190

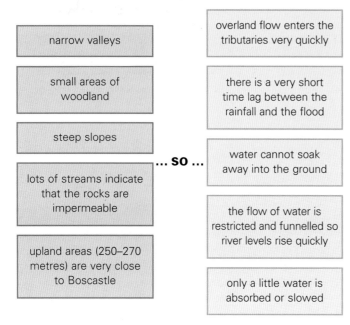

| narrow valleys |
| small areas of woodland |
| steep slopes |
| lots of streams indicate that the rocks are impermeable |
| upland areas (250–270 metres) are very close to Boscastle |

... so ...

| overland flow enters the tributaries very quickly |
| there is a very short time lag between the rainfall and the flood |
| water cannot soak away into the ground |
| the flow of water is restricted and funnelled so river levels rise quickly |
| only a little water is absorbed or slowed |

Figure 23 Reasons for the sudden rise of the River Valency during the flood in 2004

Activity

1   **a)** Match the pairs of statements shown in Figure 23 to make five sentences that help to explain how the character of this drainage basin led to the flooding in 2004.

   b) Use the OS map (Figure 22) to find five different grid squares, which provide evidence, for your five sentences. For example, you could choose 0989 to match with 'upland areas are very close to Boscastle ... so ...'

   c) Using Figure 24 as a simple outline, draw your own sketch map of the drainage basin of the River Valency. Add your five statements to appropriate places on the map as annotations.

2   Summarise how woodland areas close to the river could have affected the flood.

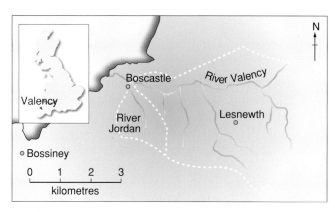

Figure 24 The drainage basin of the River Valency

Examiner's Tips

Understanding Ordnance Survey (OS) maps

You will almost certainly have an OS map resource in at least one of the questions in the examination. OS maps show the physical and human features in the British landscape. For the examination you will be expected to be able to:

- give directions
- understand grid references
- recognise symbols

- use a scale
- describe relief
- recognise patterns.

Sample question

Study Figure 22. Describe the relief in the western half of the OS map extract (west of easting 12). [5]

Student answer for Candidate A

The contour lines are close together, this shows that the area has many hills ✓ with steep slopes.✓ The highest point is 274 m.✓ The B3263 runs through. It's quite a wooded area. There are rivers flowing through the area and many deep valleys.✓

Student answer for Candidate B

The relief is hilly.✓ There is a forest and a river. The highest point in the area is 274 m.✓

What the examiner has to say!

Describe is the most commonly used command word at GCSE – you need to use lots of adjectives, e.g. high or mountainous to describe the uplands, and deep or narrow to describe the valleys. There are 5 marks available in this question so to get full marks you will need to describe five features of the relief in this section of the map. Be careful – a list is not the same as a description. Always try to develop the points that you make. For example, 'there are many hills in the west with some peaks over 250 metres high.' Candidate A scores 4 marks with four clear points made. Candidate B scores only two. Neither candidate fully understands the meaning of relief. Relief is the shape of the land which included features such as altitude, steep and gentle slopes, cliffs and valleys.

Exam practice

Study Figure 22.
1 a) What river landform is named in 1091? [1]
  b) In what general direction does the River Valency flow between Trafalgar in 1291 and its mouth in 0991? [1]
  c) What distance does the River Valency flow from its source at 152889 to its mouth at 093915? [1]
  d) Give a six figure grid reference for the telephone box in Tresparrett. [1]

2 a) Identify two map symbols which suggest that the area in Figure 22 is popular with tourists. [2]
  b) Describe the physical attractions of this area for tourism. [5]
  c) Name one group of people who may be against the use of this area for tourism and explain why they might object. [5]

13

How should rivers be managed?

How successful are different management approaches to the problem of flooding?

In the UK it is the responsibility of the Environment Agency to warn people about flood hazards and to reduce the risk of both river and coastal floods. They estimate that in England and Wales around 5 million people live in areas that are at risk of flooding.

Boscastle — Boscastle's flood defences

After the flood of 2004, the Environment Agency was responsible for designing a flood defence scheme for Boscastle. The defences cost £4.6 million and took two years to complete (2006–8). Many of the important features of this scheme are shown in Figure 25. One of the main features has been to widen and deepen the river channel so that it can carry more water. This type of river management is known as **hard engineering** as it involves artificially controlling the course of the river. Engineers were aware that during the flood the road and foot bridges in the town became blocked by large branches that had been washed downstream. They decided to deepen the river bed under the main bridge and to replace the other two bridges with new structures. These new bridges have much wider spans so it is more difficult for them to become blocked with debris.

The National Trust owns a large part of the lower section of the valley of the Valency. In the past the river was straightened and dredged so that its water could be used to power water mills. The National Trust and Environment Agency are now restoring parts of the river to take on a more natural form. For example, just before it enters the town the river has been given a wider, shallow channel. This should slow the flow of water and encourage deposition of gravel in a natural **braided** pattern. During another large flood this 'natural' section of river would help trap boulders and other load before it entered the town where it could cause damage. Using the natural features of a river in this way is known as **soft engineering**.

Wider channel

Straighter river

Figure 25 The section of river between the main bridge and the harbour has been lowered by 75 cm. The river has also been widened

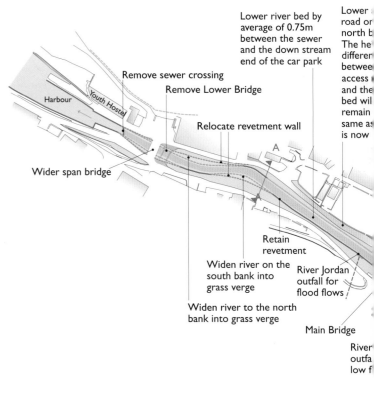

Lower river bed by average of 0.75m between the sewer and the down stream end of the car park

Lower road or north b The he differen betwee access and the bed wil remain same as is now

Remove sewer crossing

Remove Lower Bridge

Harbour

Youth Hostel

Relocate revetment wall

A

Wider span bridge

Retain revetment

Widen river on the south bank into grass verge

River Jordan outfall for flood flows

Widen river to the north bank into grass verge

Main Bridge

River outfa low f

Figure 26 A plan of the Boscastle flood defences designed by the Environment Agency and built 2006–8

Figure 27 Workmen using a JCB to dig out the rocky bed of the river under the main bridge during 2007. This is the same bridge as in Figure 17

Figure 28 One of the new footbridges and a view east along the widened river. The car park is behind the building in the left of the photo

Activity

1 Use Figure 26 to describe the flow of the River Valency through Boscastle.

2 Use Figure 26 to explain why the Bridge Walk shops were at risk during the 2004 flood.

3 Explain how each of the following features shown in Figure 26 will reduce the risk of future floods:
   a) lowering the river bed
   b) widening the river channel
   c) removal of trees next to the river
   d) replacing two of the bridges with wider spans.

4 Use Figures 25–28 to give examples of different types of:
   a) hard engineering
   b) soft engineering.

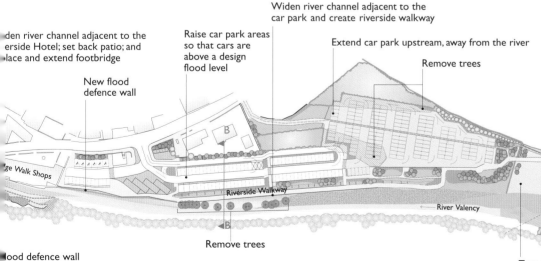

Widen river channel adjacent to the car park and create riverside walkway

den river channel adjacent to the erside Hotel; set back patio; and lace and extend footbridge

Raise car park areas so that cars are above a design flood level

Extend car park upstream, away from the river

Remove trees

New flood defence wall

B

B

Riverside Walkway

ge Walk Shops

River Valency

Remove trees

ood defence wall

Form wide, braided river channel upstream of the car park to create an area of slower flow, where larger sediment will deposit

Realign existing channel

Tree and debris catching facility

Catchment management work upstream

N   0 10   50m

Being prepared for a flood

Building flood defences is expensive and controversial. Some scientists argue that straightening rivers and building flood embankments increases the risk of flooding further downstream. In addition to building flood defences the Environment Agency believe that flood risk can be reduced by:

- encouraging homeowners and businesses to have a flood plan
- improved **weather** forecasting linked to monitoring river levels that can provide accurate flood warnings
- advising local authorities and planners about flood hazards. Encouraging only low risk land uses (such as car parks or football pitches) in areas that are at high risk of flooding.

your flood plan

Know how to turn off your gas, electricity and water mains supplies

Start preparing today before a flood happens. Use this checklist as your flood plan.

1. **Check your insurance cover**
   - Check your buildings and contents insurance policy.
   - Confirm you are covered for flooding.
   - Find out if the policy replaces new for old, and if it has a limit on repairs.
   - Don't underestimate the value of your contents.

2. **Know how to turn off your gas, electricity and water mains supplies**
   - Ask your supplier how to do this.
   - Mark taps or switches with stickers to help you remember.

3. **Prepare a flood kit of essential items** (please tick)
   - ☐ Copies of your home insurance documents.
   - ☐ A torch with spare batteries.
   - ☐ A wind-up or battery radio.
   - ☐ Warm, waterproof clothing and blankets.
   - ☐ A first aid kit and prescription medication.
   - ☐ Bottled water and non-perishable foods.
   - ☐ Baby food and baby care items.
   - ☐ This leaflet including your list of important contact numbers.
   - ☐ Keep your flood kit handy.

4. **Know who to contact and how**
   - Agree where you will go and how to contact each other.
   - Check with your council if pets are allowed at evacuation centres.
   - Keep a list with all your important contacts to hand.

5. **Think about what you can move now**
   - Don't wait for a flood. Move items of personal value such as photo albums, family videos and treasured mementos to a safe place.

6. **Think about what you would want to move to safety during a flood**
   - Outdoor pets
   - Cars
   - Furniture
   - Electrical equipment
   - Garden pot plants and furniture
   - What else? ....
   ....

Figure 29 Screenshot from the Environment Agency website showing 'Your flood plan'

Shrewsbury. Flood damage in 1998, 2000, 2002 and 2004. The severe floods of 2000 led to the construction of flood defences completed in spring 2007.

Bewdley. Flood damage in 1998, 2000 and 2002. Flood defences (including demountable barriers in Figure 31) were completed before the February 2004 flood.

Tewkesbury is on the confluence of the River Avon and River Severn. Both Tewkesbury and **Gloucester** were badly affected by the floods in 2000 and 2007.

Figure 30 Recent floods on the River Severn

The tops of iron railings that are under the flood water.

Demountable pillars fitted into sockets in the top of a flood wall just before the flood.

Aluminium shuttering has been slotted into the pillars.

Figure 31 Demountable flood barriers (also known as invisible flood defences) being used in Bewdley for the first time during the February 2004 flood

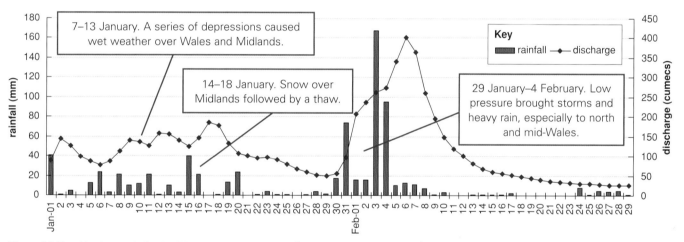

7–13 January. A series of depressions caused wet weather over Wales and Midlands.

14–18 January. Snow over Midlands followed by a thaw.

29 January–4 February. Low pressure brought storms and heavy rain, especially to north and mid-Wales.

Key
▨ rainfall ◆ discharge

Figure 32 Flood hydrograph for the River Severn at Bewdley (January–February 2004). Rainfall data is for Capel Curig, North Wales

Activity

1 For each of the six points in the flood plan (Figure 29) explain how they might reduce the losses suffered during a flood.

2 Describe the course of the River Severn.

3 Study Figure 32.
   a) Describe how each of the weather events described in the labels affected the flow of the river.
   b) Carefully describe the shape of the flood hydrograph between 29 January and 29 February. Make sure you use terms such as lag time and peak discharge in your answer.
   c) Use Figures 30 and 32 to suggest how the Environment Agency uses rainfall data from Wales to predict flood events in Bewdley.

Geography Futures

Should we change our approach to river and floodplain management in the future?

In 2004 the UK government commissioned a scientific report on the future of river and coastal floods in the UK. The scientists considered how climate change and growing populations might affect the risk of flooding by the year 2080. The main findings of the 'Futures Report' are:

- The number of people at high risk of flooding could rise from 1.5 million to 3.5 million.
- The economic cost of flood damage will rise. At the moment flooding costs the UK £1 billion a year. By 2080 it could cost as much as £27 billion.
- One of the main causes of the extra flood risk is climate change. The UK's climate is likely to become stormier with more frequent heavy rain. Sea level rise will increase the risk of coastal floods.
- About 10 per cent of the UK's housing is already built on the floodplains of rivers and these homes are at risk of river floods. Hundreds of thousands of new houses will be built in the next 20 years and many of these could also be at risk.
- River floods could cause massive health risks if the flood water contains untreated sewage or chemicals that have been washed off farm land.
- Towns and cities will be at risk of flash floods even if they are not built near a river. Drains that are supposed to carry away rainwater will not be able to cope with sudden downpours of rain. This kind of flooding could affect as many as 710,000 people.

Activity

1 Use Figure 33 to describe the distribution of areas where there are high numbers of people at risk of flooding.

2 Describe how future floods are likely to affect people living:
   a) in coastal areas
   b) close to rivers
   c) in towns and cities.

3 What are the main reasons for extra flood hazards in the future?

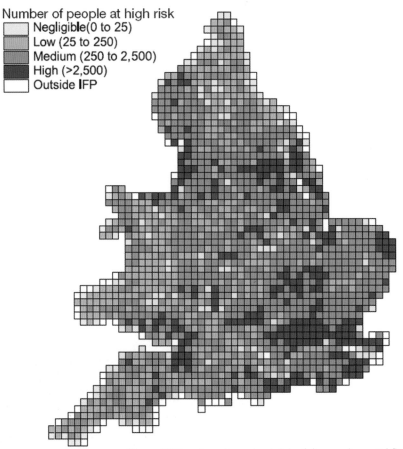

Figure 33 Number of people at risk of river and coastal floods in 2080 assuming that carbon dioxide emissions remain high

The report suggests that the flood risk has been made worse by building towns too close to rivers. A lot of homes are at risk because they have been built on floodplains. Furthermore, large areas of concrete and tarmac are impermeable and cause increased overland flow. If it weren't for storm drains under the street, city roads would be covered in deep puddles every time it rains. However, during long and intense periods of rain these storm drains cannot always cope. The water comes back out of the drain and floods the city. This is what happened in the floods in Hull in June 2007. The government has set a housing target of building three million new homes by 2020. What affect might all of this building have on future floods?

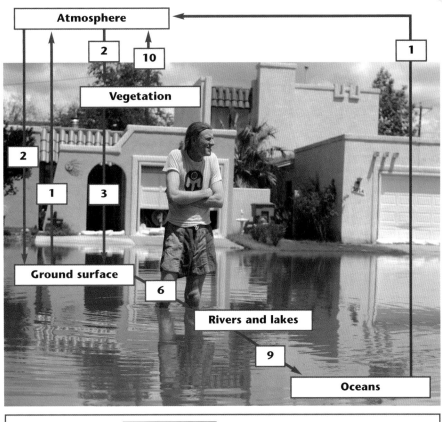

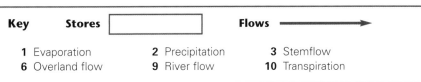

Key	Stores			Flows	
	1 Evaporation		**2** Precipitation		**3** Stemflow
	6 Overland flow		**9** River flow		**10** Transpiration

Figure 34 Stores and flows of water in an urban drainage basin

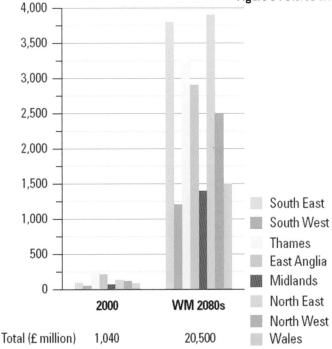

Total (£ million)   1,040   20,500

Figure 35 Possible increase in economic costs of coastal and river floods (worst case scenario) for regions of England and Wales

South East
South West
Thames
East Anglia
Midlands
North East
North West
Wales

Activity

4 Compare Figure 34 with Figure 18 (on page 9)
   a) Describe the similarities and differences between these diagrams.
   b) Use the differences to explain why an urban area would be more at risk from flooding than a forested drainage basin.

5 a) Use Figure 35 to estimate the economic cost of flooding in each region.
   b) The government says that three million new homes are needed. Many are planned for the Thames and South East regions. What would you recommend should be done if these new houses are built?

Geography Futures

What should be done to reduce the risk of future floods?

Planner

Householders should be encouraged not to pave over their gardens. Paving and tarmac are impermeable. Rainwater goes straight down into storm drains and into the river rather than soaking slowly into the soil. Advice needs to be given so that gravel and permeable surfaces are used instead of tarmac. We also need to replace old storm drains which are too old and small to cope with heavy rain storms. However, motorists won't like that because it will mean digging up urban roads!

The scientists who wrote the 'Futures Report' into flooding identified that poor land management had increased the risk of river floods. For example, over the last 50 years farmers in upland areas of England and Wales have added drains to their fields to improve the amount of grass that can be grown. However, these field drains have had an effect on the flow of rivers further downstream. We are involved in a scheme to restore the old peat bogs in upland Wales. Between 2006 and 2011 we are going to block a total of 90 km of old land drains on the hills close to Lake Vyrnwy. We are using bales made from heather to block the drains. This will slow down the overland flow and force water to soak back into the soil. Not only will this help reduce the risk of floods but it will also improve the moorland ecosystem and will help to protect rare birds of prey like the merlin and hen harrier.

Spokesperson for RSPB

River scientist

Hard engineering schemes, like the flood walls and embankments in Shrewsbury, speed up the flow of water. These schemes may funnel water along to the next community living further downstream and actually increase their risk of flooding. What we need to do is to return river valleys to a more natural state. We should use floodplains as temporary water stores so that flooding can occur away from built-up areas.

Homes can be made more flood proof with measures such as putting plug sockets higher up the walls and using yacht varnish to make wooden floors waterproof.

House builder

Resident in Shrewsbury

I'm really pleased with the new flood defences. My property has flooded in the past but was protected during 2007. The Shrewsbury flood defence scheme cost £4.6 million but I think it was worth it.

We need to build an extra 3 million homes in the UK by 2020. Almost half of them are in the Midlands and the south of England which are the same areas hit by flooding in 2007. Some of these houses will have to be built on greenfield sites. However, we should restrict building on floodplains in the future.

Government housing minister

Figure 36 Alternative points of view on solving the flood problem

a) The natural system

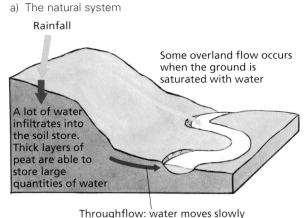

b) Field drains were added to improve grazing

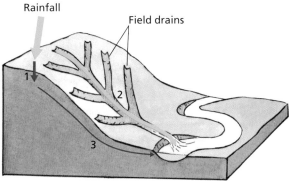

Figure 37 The movement of water through upland drainage basins was altered when field drains were added. The size of the arrows is in proportion to the amount of each flow

Activity

1 Study Figure 37.
   a) Make a copy of diagram b. Add labels that explain water flows at 1, 2 and 3.
   b) Explain how the differences in the two diagrams would affect the flow of water in the river downstream.

2 You have been asked to advise Tewksbury Council on flood prevention. What do you think should be done to prevent future floods in the town?
   a) Use what you have learned in this chapter, and the points of view in Figure 36 to complete a copy of the table.

Possible solution	Short-term benefits and problems	Long-term benefits and problems	Who might agree and disagree with this solution
Building flood defences like those in Shrewsbury			
Restoring bogs and moorland in mid-Wales by blocking drains			
Tighter controls on building on floodplains and paving over gardens			
Allowing rivers to flow naturally and spill over on to the floodplain			

   b) Now you need to recommend your plan. What do you think should be done and why do you think your plan will work? Use the following table to plan your answer.

Key questions to ask yourself	My answers
Is my plan realistic, affordable and achievable?	
Which groups of people will benefit from my plan?	
How will the environment be affected?	
Why is this plan better than the alternatives?	

GIS Activity: The Environment Agency

Using the Environment Agency website

www.environment-agency.gov.uk

The Environment Agency operates a simple GIS that shows flood hazards. Follow the weblink above and click on 'Flood map and how to use it' within the 'Prepare for Flooding' section. You can now search the atlas using postcodes. Figure 38 shows that central Tewkesbury is at risk of being surrounded by water from the rivers Avon and Severn during a flood.

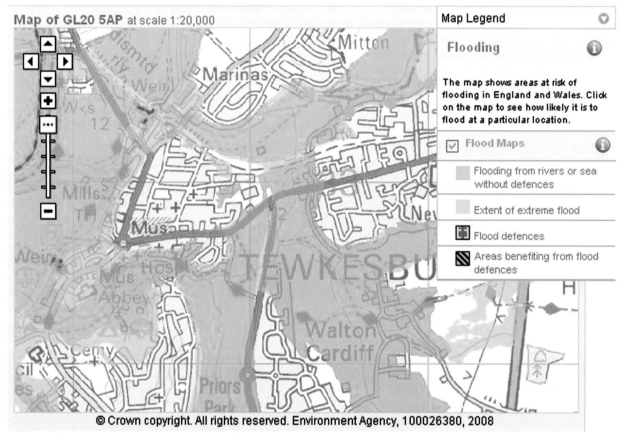

Map of GL20 5AP at scale 1:20,000

Map Legend

Flooding

The map shows areas at risk of flooding in England and Wales. Click on the map to see how likely it is to flood at a particular location.

☑ Flood Maps

Flooding from rivers or sea without defences

Extent of extreme flood

Flood defences

Areas benefiting from flood defences

© Crown copyright. All rights reserved. Environment Agency, 100026380, 2008

Figure 38 A screenshot for the Environment Agency flood maps GIS

Activity

1 Use the following postcodes to examine the flood risk to towns along the River Severn (the postcodes are in order going from source to mouth)
   SY16 2LN   SY21 7DG   SY3 8HQ   DY12 2AE   GL20 5AP
   a) For each town identify:
      i) the extent (area) that is at risk
      ii) which main roads are at risk of flooding
      iii) whether residential areas are at risk or not
      iv) whether the town has any flood defences.
   b) Based on your findings, suggest which of these towns most needs new flood defences.

What are the causes and evidence for climate change?

The drought in Australia between 2002 and 2008 has been described as the worst drought to affect the country for 1000 years.

Are extreme weather events like this evidence of climate change?

How might climate change in the future?

What can we do to reduce the effects of climate change?

Figure 1 Forest fires burning close to Sydney, Australia, January 2003. Widespread forest fires in February 2009 in the state of Victoria killed over 200 people

What is the greenhouse effect?

The greenhouse effect is a natural process of our atmosphere. Without it, the average surface temperature of the Earth would be −17 Celsius rather than the 15 Celsius we currently experience. At these temperatures life would not have evolved on Earth in its present form and we probably wouldn't exist!

The greenhouse effect, shown in Figure 2, means that Earth's atmosphere acts like an insulating blanket. Light (short wave) and heat (long wave) energy from the sun pass through the atmosphere quite easily. The sun's energy heats the Earth and it radiates its own energy back into the atmosphere. The long-wave heat energy coming from the Earth is quite easily absorbed by naturally occurring gases in the atmosphere. These are known as **greenhouse gases.** They include carbon dioxide (CO_2), methane (CH_4) and water vapour (H_2O). Carbon dioxide is the fourth most common gas in the atmosphere. It occurs naturally in the atmosphere as a product of respiration from all living things. So carbon dioxide has existed in the atmosphere for as long as there has been life on Earth. Methane and water vapour have been in the atmosphere for even longer, so the greenhouse effect has been affecting our climate for thousands of millions of years.

Activity

1 Use Figure 2 to explain the greenhouse effect.

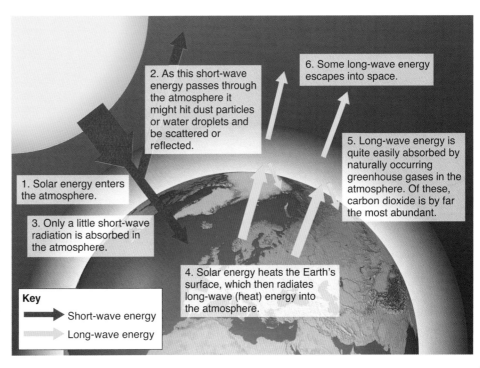

2. As this short-wave energy passes through the atmosphere it might hit dust particles or water droplets and be scattered or reflected.

6. Some long-wave energy escapes into space.

5. Long-wave energy is quite easily absorbed by naturally occurring greenhouse gases in the atmosphere. Of these, carbon dioxide is by far the most abundant.

1. Solar energy enters the atmosphere.

3. Only a little short-wave radiation is absorbed in the atmosphere.

4. Solar energy heats the Earth's surface, which then radiates long-wave (heat) energy into the atmosphere.

Key
→ Short-wave energy
→ Long-wave energy

Figure 2 The greenhouse effect

How have people's actions affected the greenhouse effect?

Carbon is one of the most common elements in the environment. It is present in:

- all organic substances, i.e. all living things
- simple compounds such as CO_2, which exists as a gas in the atmosphere and is dissolved in the oceans
- complex compounds, for example hydrocarbons found in fossil fuels such as oil, coal and gas.

Carbon is able to transfer from one part of the environment to another through a series of biological processes, such as respiration, and chemical processes such as **solution**. These transfers take place between parts of the environment that release carbon, known as sources, and parts of the environment that absorb the carbon over long periods of time, known as carbon sinks. The transfer between sources and sinks is shown in the carbon cycle diagrams, Figures 3 and 4.

Figure 3 A simplified carbon cycle

At night photosynthesis stops. The tree continues to respire and it emits more CO_2 than it absorbs

Solar energy

Whilst the tree is alive it absorbs more CO_2 from the atmosphere than it emits

When branches or leaves fall they transfer the carbon that is locked in the plant tissue into the soil

During the day the tree uses sunlight to convert carbon dioxide to plant sugars. This is **photosynthesis**

Organisms such as beetles and earthworms may digest the plant tissue. Their respiration adds CO_2 to air in the soil

Rainwater dissolves some of the carbon dioxide that has come from soil organisms. This water may carry the dissolved CO_2 into a river and eventually to the sea.

Figure 4 The carbon cycle, showing fast and slow transfers

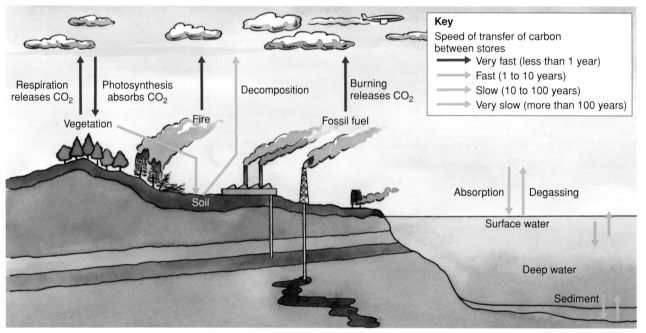

Respiration releases CO_2

Photosynthesis absorbs CO_2

Decomposition

Burning releases CO_2

Key
Speed of transfer of carbon between stores
→ Very fast (less than 1 year)
→ Fast (1 to 10 years)
→ Slow (10 to 100 years)
⇢ Very slow (more than 100 years)

Vegetation

Fire

Fossil fuel

Soil

Absorption Degassing

Surface water

Deep water

Sediment

Activity

1 Study Figures 3 and 4.
   a) Describe the human actions that release CO_2 into the atmosphere.
   b) Explain the processes that allow forests to act as a carbon sink.
   c) Give two reasons why the burning of tropical rainforests will increase the amount of CO_2 in the atmosphere.

2 Use Figure 4.
   a) Describe the difference in the speed of transfer of carbon in the natural part of the cycle compared with the part of the cycle affected by human action.
   b) Explain what difference this makes to the amount of carbon stored in the atmosphere compared with the long-lasting carbon sinks. Explain why this is alarming.

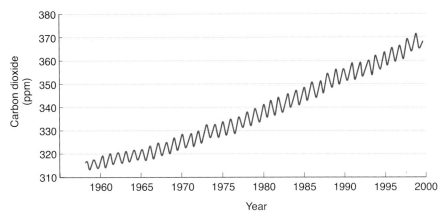

Figure 5 The Keeling Curve shows the rise of carbon dioxide in the atmosphere since monitoring began in 1958 (ppm = parts per million)

In 1958 a team of scientists began to take regular measurements of carbon dioxide concentrations from the atmosphere. They realised that local levels of CO_2 could be higher if the sampling took place close to industry or traffic congestion. So they decided to conduct their tests on Mauna Loa, Hawaii. They thought that this would give them readings that would represent average CO_2 levels in the atmosphere. The sampling has been conducted regularly ever since and the graph, known as the Keeling Curve, is shown in Figure 5.

Recent scientific research in Antarctica and Greenland (see pages 26–27) suggests that natural levels of carbon dioxide in the atmosphere vary between 180 ppm and 280 ppm. However, the current concentration of CO_2 in the atmosphere is around 380 ppm. This increase is largely due to human actions that have disturbed the natural processes of the carbon cycle.

The destruction and burning of forests, first in Europe and now in tropical regions, releases huge amounts of CO_2 from trees into the atmosphere. Our reliance on fossil fuels to create heat and energy over the last 200 years has also released large quantities of CO_2 into the atmosphere. The emission of CO_2 and other greenhouse gases has thrown the global carbon cycle out of balance. Carbon has been taken from long-term sinks, such as fossil fuels that were buried in the ground, and been transferred into the atmosphere. With more gases able to absorb and trap heat, the greenhouse effect has become stronger. This is what we call the **enhanced greenhouse effect** and most scientists agree it has lead to a **global warming** of the atmosphere.

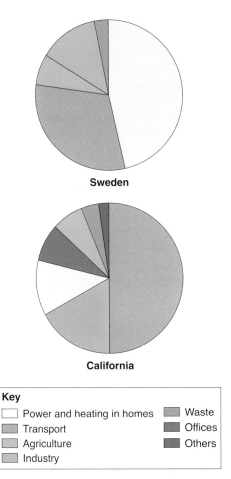

Figure 6 The source of greenhouse gases in Sweden and California, USA

Activity

3 **a)** Make a copy of Figure 2.
   b) Label your copy of the diagram to show how the enhanced greenhouse effect works. Think carefully about which of the six labels you will need to alter.

4 **a)** Describe and explain the trend of the Keeling Curve.
   b) Explain why the scientists chose Hawaii as a good place to collect their samples.

5 Use Figure 6.
   a) Compare the source of emissions in Sweden and California.
   b) Suggests reasons for these differences.
   c) Suggest how these pie charts might be different if they were for a **Less Economically Developed Country (LEDC)** such as Mali or Niger in Africa.

How conclusive is the evidence for climate change?

The majority of climate scientists (climatologists) now agree that people's actions are contributing to global climate change. They believe that extra greenhouse gases are warming the atmosphere and that this is changing the global climate at a pace that is quite unlike any natural cycle. There are many separate pieces of evidence for climate change caused by humans. They are rather like the pieces of a jigsaw. Each piece of evidence is not really conclusive on its own. However, when we look at the big picture it is clear that all the pieces of the jigsaw fit together to make a convincing and persuasive argument.

Evidence from the ice cores

We have already seen that scientific evidence from Hawaii proves that carbon dioxide levels have been rising steadily since 1958. However, can we be certain that this isn't part of a natural cycle? Perhaps carbon dioxide levels vary over long periods of time and the recent rise is part of one of those cycles.

Scientists working in both Greenland and Antarctica have been investigating information trapped in the ice to uncover evidence of past climate change. The snowfall from each winter is covered over and compressed by the following winter's snowfall. Each layer of snow contains chemical evidence about the temperature of the climate. Each layer also contains trapped gases from the atmosphere that the snow fell through. Gradually the layers turn to ice. Over thousands of years these layers have built up and are now 1000s of metres thick. By drilling down into the ice, scientists can extract older and older ice cores. Chemical analysis of these ice layers and the gases they contain reveal a record of the climate over the last 420,000 years. This evidence suggests that the climate has indeed gone through natural cycles of colder (**glacials**) and warmer periods (**interglacials**). They also show that levels of carbon dioxide in the atmosphere have also gone up and down as part of a natural cycle.

Figure 7 Scientists taking ice core samples from the ice sheet in Greenland

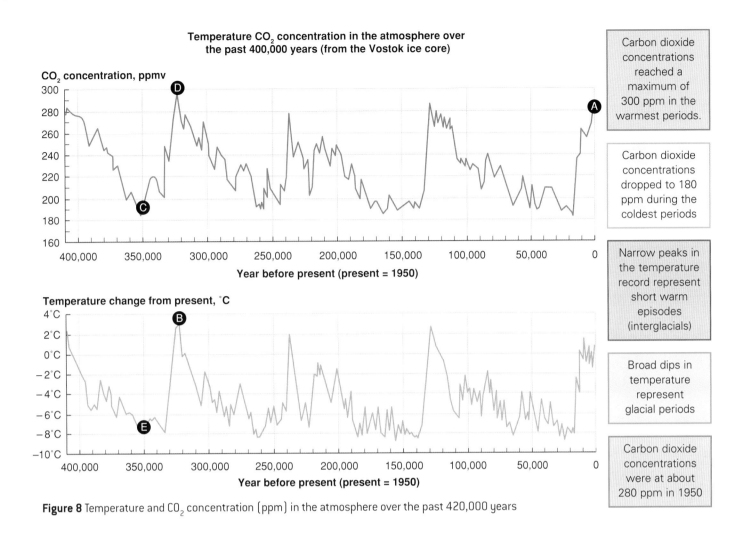

Figure 8 Temperature and CO_2 concentration (ppm) in the atmosphere over the past 420,000 years

Activity

1 Use Figure 8.
   a) Match the five statements to the correct place on the graph shown by the letters A, B, C, D and E.
   b) Use the graph to copy and complete the following statement:
      The graph shows natural cycles of …………. periods and ………… periods. Average temperatures were higher than present on *three / four / five* occasions. These are known as …………. periods. The current interglacial period appears to have lasted *much longer than/shorter than* previous periods.

2 Use your understanding of the greenhouse effect to explain why reduced levels of carbon dioxide in the atmosphere might be linked to cooler periods of climate.

3 Compare Figure 8 with Figure 5.
   a) How many times in the last 420,000 years have CO_2 levels been as high as in 2000?
   b) Based on the ice core data, do you think that the Keeling Curve fits into a similar natural cycle of carbon dioxide concentrations? Explain your answer fully.

4 How conclusive do you find the evidence for:
   a) natural cycles of climate change over the last 420,000 years?
   b) an unusual rise in carbon dioxide levels since 1958?

Iceland

Evidence from recent weather observations

What's the difference between weather and climate? Weather is our day-to-day experience of temperature, wind, rainfall and sunshine. **Climate** is about taking weather readings over long periods of time, and then working out averages, patterns and trends. One effect of climate change is that extreme weather events are likely to get more common in the future. So do recent weather records show any evidence that the weather is getting more extreme?

Iceland is located in the North Atlantic just south of the Arctic Circle. The mean temperature (taken as an average over the whole year) is 3.5 Celsius in Stykkisholmur which is a small fishing port on the west coast. The mean July and August temperatures here are just below 10 Celsius. Leisure time is influenced by the cool climate. Swimming and bathing in the natural hot springs are enjoyed by many people whereas relaxing on the beach is almost unknown. However, in July 2008 Iceland experienced its hottest summer on record. Is this kind of extreme weather event evidence of climate change?

Activity

1 Use Figures 10 and 11.
   a) How much warmer was Iceland in July 2008 than average?
   b) Why does the author of the weblog feel sorry for people from Iceland who had gone abroad for their holiday?

2 Use the evidence from this page to explain the difference between weather and climate.

3 a) Study Figures 10 and 11. How conclusive do you find this as evidence for climate change?
   b) Now examine Figure 12. Is this evidence more or less convincing? Explain your answer carefully.

Figure 9 Citizens of Reykjavik visiting the Nauthólsvik thermal beach in August 2005

The weather here has been amazing over the past 2–3 weeks and yesterday was a perfect gem in the string of beautiful days we've had here lately. We had record highs throughout the country – here in Reykjavík temps went up to 26.2 °C, breaking the previous record of 24.8 °C. At Thingvellir temps were 29.7 °C, which was also a record and was HIGHER THAN IN THE ALGARVE in Portugal (pity the poor Icelanders who spent tens of thousands of their hard-earned crowns to holiday there in the sun). There was brilliant sunshine all day long and a deliciously warm wind, which hardly EVER happens here.

Figure 10 Extract from an Icelander's weblog

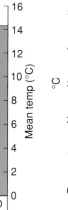

Figure 11 Climate graph for Stykkisholmur on the west coast of Iceland

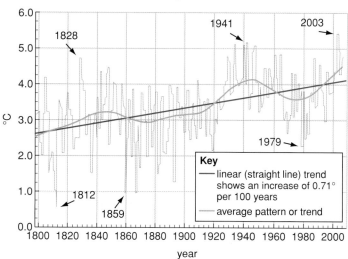

Figure 12 Annual temperature in Stykkisholmur 1798 to 2007

Describing graphs

Graphs are used to present data and to identify patterns and trends. You will be expected to understand, interpret and perhaps add data to a range of different tables, charts and graphs. These include:

- line graphs
- bar graphs
- pie charts
- scattergraphs
- pictograms.

Sample question

Study Figure 12 on page 28.

(a) Describe the trend in annual temperature in Stykkisholmur between 1798 and 2007. [4]

(b) Give possible reasons to explain this trend. [5]

Student answer

(a) The trend of the graph shows the annual temperature increases✓. It does not rise at a steady rate✓ as the annual temperature starts to drop in 1845 then rises again and drops again in 1950✓. The temperature has increased on average from 2.5°C to over 4°C✓. It was at its highest in 2003 at 5.4°C✓.

(b) The temperature rise is due to global warming which is caused by an increase in carbon dioxide✓ emissions. Also more electricity✓ is used as the centuries have passed. The heat melts the ice caps as it is prevented from escaping raising the temperature of Iceland. Another process over the years is deforestation✓ and there are not enough trees to absorb the carbon dioxide✓.

What the examiner has to say!

(a) This is a good answer. The candidate has described the overall trend, noted variations in this trend and quoted figures from the graph. Full marks!

(b) *Explain* is a common command word – you need to account for or say why something is happening. In this answer the candidate has understood the command word but lacks detailed knowledge. Melting ice caps is relevant but the candidate fails to make the connection between this factor and rising temperatures – hence there in no explanation. The candidate develops a mark for deforestation into 2 marks by explaining its importance. This answer is worth 4 marks, not containing enough detail to achieve the 5 marks available for this question.

Exam practice

1. Study Figure 11 on page 28
a) What is the annual range of temperature in Stykkisholmur? (Find the mean maximum and minimum temperature in the year and then find the difference.) [2]
b) Describe the trend in temperature throughout the year in Stykkisholmur. [4]
c) What is the total annual rainfall in Stykkisholmur? (Add together the monthly precipitation totals.) [1]
d) Give possible reasons to explain the climate of Stykkisholmur. [5]

2. Use the information in the table to answer the following questions.
a) Plot line graphs to show the changes in carbon dioxide levels and temperatures in the last 200 years. [4]
b) Describe the pattern each graph shows. [4]
c) Plot a scattergraph of carbon dioxide (x axis) against temperature (y axis). (Scattergraphs are used to show the relationship between two sets of data. Draw a best fit line to show the trend). [4]
d) Describe the relationship between carbon dioxide in the atmosphere and mean annual temperature differences (note any anomalies). [4]

Year	1800	1820	1840	1860	1880	1900	1920	1940	1960	1980	2000
CO_2 levels in parts per million	282	284	285	286	290	296	302	310	321	340	370
Mean annual temperature in °C	−0.9	−0.95	−0.8	−0.7	−0.45	−0.4	−0.2	0	0.05	0.3	0.7

Warning signs from nature

A number of ecologists (scientists who study plants and animals) are beginning to contribute to the debate on climate change. They argue that some wildlife is very sensitive to climate change so that small changes in temperature or rainfall can cause noticeable changes in behaviour or distribution. If the ecologists are right, then this kind of evidence would be another piece of the jigsaw. One such piece of evidence comes from scientists studying polar bears in Hudson Bay, Canada.

There are about 20,000 polar bears living in the Arctic and 1,200 of these live in the Hudson Bay region. Polar bears are at the top of the Arctic food chain. They hunt on the frozen sea ice in spring and feed on newly born seals during March and April. This period is critical for the bears. They may put on between 50 per cent and 75 per cent of their body fat during these few weeks. After the ice thaws they will eat very little until the sea ice returns in autumn. Studies made by the Canadian Wildlife Service show that the ice in Hudson Bay now melts three weeks earlier than it did when studies began in the early 1970s. For each week that the thaw comes early, the bears have less chance to feed, and they come on shore 10 kg lighter. The consequences of further climate change are worrying.

- More young bears and pups will starve over the longer summer.
- Females will be less fertile.
- Hungry bears are more likely to forage for food in towns where they come into conflict with people.

Figure 13 Distribution of polar bears and location of Hudson Bay

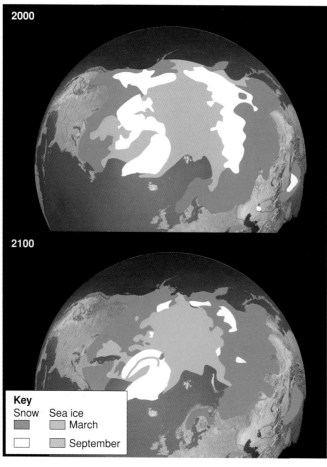

Key

Snow

Sea ice

☐ March

☐ September

Figure 14 The extent of sea ice in 2000 compared with the predicted extent in 2100

Activity

1 Study Figure 13.
   a) Describe the location of Hudson Bay.
   b) Describe the distribution of polar bears.

2 Use Figures 13 and 14.
   a) Compare the distribution of polar bears with the sea ice in March 2000.
   b) Describe what is predicted to happen to the sea ice in March 2100.
   c) Explain fully how the changing pattern of sea ice shown in Figure 14 could affect the population of polar bears.

3 Explain why studies of animal behaviour over several years could provide more conclusive evidence of climate change than simply recording temperature readings.

GIS Activity: British wildlife study – Nature's Calendar

www.naturescalendar.org.uk

Figure 15 The logos of the Nature's Calendar website and the Woodland Trust

The Woodland Trust run a survey that asks the public to send in sightings of seasonal events where they live. Thousands of people take part and the Nature's Calendar survey has collected observations of natural events as far back as the 1600s. The Nature's Calendar website allows you to record your sightings of significant wildlife events in both spring and autumn, for example, the arrival of the first swallow, or the first frogspawn. The results are displayed on animated maps.

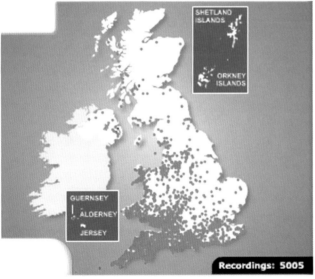

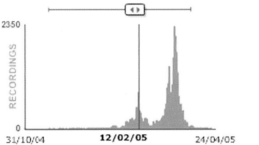

Figure 16 The screenshot shows an example of one of the interactive maps available on the site. This one shows first sightings of frogspawn up until 12 February 2005. Notice that the graph shows sightings of frogspawn reported each day up until 24 April 2005.

Activity

1 **a)** Describe the distribution of sightings of frogspawn on the map.
   b) Suggest reasons why frogspawn is seen earlier in some parts of the UK than others.

2 Work in pairs. If you have access to the internet, log on to the site.
   a) Discuss how you could use the site to compare the progress of spring in different years.
   b) Suggest a hypothesis linking evidence on the site to climate change, e.g. **If climate change is making winters milder then I would expect to see ....**
   c) Test your hypothesis and present a short presentation to your class of your findings.

What are the alternative futures?

What are the possible effects of climate change on MEDCs and LEDCs?

Global changes in the climate due to greenhouse gas emissions are likely to have a wide variety of impacts and some places could be worse hit than others.

In 2005, New Orleans was flooded by a storm surge of water created by Hurricane Katrina. A total of 1,836 people were killed by Katrina. Much of the city is built below sea level. The city is built on the soft sands of a river delta and as these dry out the city gradually sinks. This subsidence, combined with rising sea levels, means that New Orleans is at increasing risk of more floods.

About 3.6 billion people (or 60 per cent of the world's population) live within 60 km of the coast. This is likely to rise to 6.4 billion (75 per cent of the world's population) by 2030.

Between 1900 and 2000 the world's sea levels rose on average by 2 mm per year. This is mainly due to the melting of ice on the world's continents, especially in Greenland and Antarctica.

Of the world's 23 mega-cities, sixteen are in coastal regions and are at risk from further sea-level rise. Many of these cities are in Less Economically Developed Countries (LEDCs) and are continuing to grow rapidly. This photograph was taken in Mumbai, the world's second largest city, during the floods in August 2005.

If greenhouse emissions continue at their present rate it is likely that sea levels will continue to rise by, on average, 4 mm a year over the next 100 years.

The Thames flood barrier was completed in 1982 to protect London from tidal surges of water coming up the river from the North Sea. Tide levels are rising in the Thames estuary by about 6 mm per year (60 cm in 100 years). A major flood would perhaps cause damage to the value of £30,000 million and would certainly cause many deaths.

What will be the impact on the billions of people living in coastal regions?

Figure 17 The impact of climate change on coastal populations

Category 5: Over 250 kph. Complete failure of some smaller buildings. Failure of the roofs of large industrial buildings. Extensive coastal flooding damages the ground floor of many buildings.

Category 4: 211–250 kph. Complete destruction of the roofs of smaller buildings and more extensive damage to the walls. All signs and trees are blown down. Flooding of coastal areas 3 to 5 hours before the arrival of the storm may cut off escape routes.

Category 3: 178–210 kph. Severe damage to the roofs of small buildings. Some structural damage to walls. Mobile homes destroyed. Poorly constructed road signs destroyed. Large trees blown down.

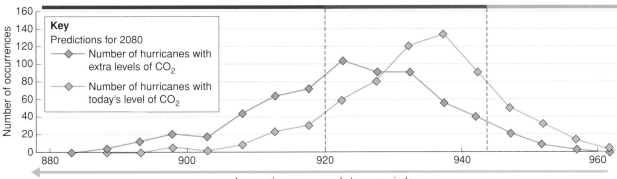

The strongest hurricanes in the present climate may be upstaged by even more intense hurricanes over the next century as the Earth's climate is warmed by increasing levels of greenhouse gases in the atmosphere. Although we cannot say at present whether more or fewer hurricanes will occur in the future with global warming, the hurricanes that do occur near the end of the 21st century are expected to be stronger and have significantly more intense rainfall than under present-day climate conditions.

Figure 18 The National Oceanic and Atmosphere Administration (NOAA) has used computer models to predict frequency and intensity of hurricanes in 2080

Activity

1 Outline how climate change could affect people living in coastal areas.

2 Study Figure 18. Describe how the frequency and violence of hurricanes are expected to change.

3 a) Use the data in Figure 20 to produce a graph of closures.
   b) Describe the trend of your graph.
   c) Explain how this graph could be seen to be more evidence for climate change.

4 Use evidence from pages 30–33 to explain why global warming is an 'issue of international concern'.

5 Suggest why people living in cities in **More Economically Developed Countries (MEDC)** may be able to cope with climate change and extreme weather better than people living in LEDC cities.

'The potential for fairly significant rises in temperature in Arctic regions seems to be quite high. And should that happen, especially over a time scale of decades, the possibility of marine mammals being able to adapt rapidly enough is very low.'

Figure 19 The opinion of Dr Malcolm Ramsay, Professor of Biology at the University of Saskatchewan, Canada

Year	Number of closures
1983	1
1984	0
1985	0
1986	0
1987	1
1988	1
1989	0
1990	3
1991	0
1992	1
1993	5
1994	1
1995	3
1996	4
1997	0
1998	3
1999	3
2000	6
2001	11
2002	2
2003	8
2004	2
2005	5
2006	1
2007	11

Figure 20 Closures of the Thames barrier to protect against storm (tidal) surges (1983–2007)

How will climate change affect Iceland?

The Arctic is one region where climate change is predicted to have a huge impact. Iceland's landscape will certainly change as its ice caps and glaciers melt. However, in the short term the economy could benefit as melting glaciers feed Iceland's rivers and these provide hydro-electric power (HEP) for Iceland's industry. Run-off from glaciers will peak sometime in the next 30 years and, according to computer models, Iceland's glaciers will have disappeared by 2200.

Will people still want to visit this wilderness region?

What will happen to the ice and to this river?

How will climate change affect this landscape?

Figure 21 Fording the rivers of central Iceland can only be attempted during July and August

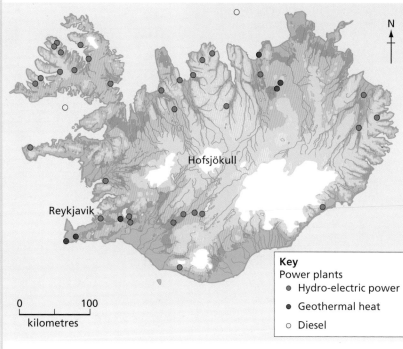

Key
Power plants
- Hydro-electric power
- Geothermal heat
- ○ Diesel

Hofsjökull

Reykjavik

0   100
kilometres

Figure 22 Iceland's power stations

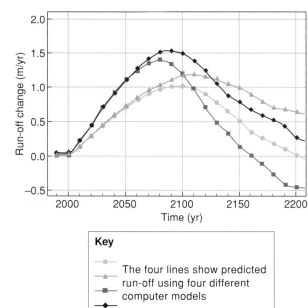

Key

The four lines show predicted run-off using four different computer models

Figure 23 Predicted changes in run-off (river discharge) from Hofsjökull ice cap in central Iceland. The lines show predicted run-off compared with averages in the year 2000

Between 1570 and 1890 Iceland's climate was at least 1 °Celsius cooler than today. Sea ice came down from the Arctic and surrounded Iceland making it difficult to bring fishing boats onshore. Glaciers expanded and covered some farms. Grain and hay crops failed and there was famine. If the temperature rises 1°Celsius above today's temperature then farmers will be able to start growing wheat. They will also greatly increase the number of cattle and sheep they keep because they will be able to grow 20 per cent more hay.

We are obviously concerned about the negative impacts of climate change. Most of the 300,000 people in Iceland live close to the coast. Sea level rise will threaten Reykjavik and other, smaller towns. Extreme weather events caused by low pressure will become more common. Storm surges will cause coastal erosion and flooding. Of greatest concern is the future of the fishing industry which is so important to our economy. Even small changes in the ocean currents could affect fish stocks in the seas around Iceland but the scientific predictions on this are still unclear.

Climate expert

Spokesperson for a power company

Government spokesperson

Tour rep

Around 87 per cent of Iceland's electricity is generated by HEP stations (and most of the rest comes from other renewables, particularly geothermal power). The construction of a new dam at Kárahnjúkar in east Iceland has been criticised by environmentalists. They don't like the loss of wilderness. But I say that Iceland is creating clean energy because we do not rely on fossil fuels. Climate change will gradually cause the glaciers and ice caps to melt. This means that rivers will have even greater discharges during the spring and summer months. We will be able to create even more electricity. That will make Iceland an even bigger attraction to energy hungry industries such as aluminium smelting and web servers.

Iceland's tourist industry has grown rapidly in the last 20 years. Most tourists arrive by air but environmental campaigners criticise air travel saying that it causes CO_2 emissions. They say flying should cost more. Will people still come here if the cost of flying becomes more expensive? Something else worries me. Most tourists come here to see our beautiful landscape and wilderness areas. Will people still visit Iceland if there is no ice?

Figure 24 Differing viewpoints on climate change in Iceland

Activity

1   Discuss Figure 21. List the changes you might expect to this landscape in 30 years' time and in 200 years' time.

2   **a)** Describe the location of the Hofsjökull ice cap.
    b) Describe the distribution of:
        i) geothermal power stations
        ii) HEP stations.

3   Use Figure 23 to predict what might happen to Iceland's production of HEP by 2050, 2100 and 2200. Explain why Iceland's energy companies need to find alternative sources of power.

4   **a)** Use the views in Figure 24 to complete the following table.

Short-term changes	Longer-term changes
Views that are generally positive	
Views that are generally negative	

   b) Use your completed table to explain what you would do if you were in government in Iceland to try to create a sustainable future for your country.

Geography Futures

What are the possible effects of climate change on LEDCs?

Climate change is likely to have a serious impact on people and environments in Africa. More frequent extreme weather events, increased temperatures and more irregular patterns of rainfall will have effects on crop production, which in turn could damage some economies and cause food shortages. It is also likely that the mosquitoes that carry malaria will move into new regions so that the number of people at risk of infection will increase. Perhaps the largest concern is that the number of people who suffer from **water stress** (i.e. do not have access to enough fresh water) will increase. There are currently 1.7 billion people worldwide who suffer from water stress. Most of these are in Africa. As the population grows and the climate changes it is expected that this number will rise to 5 billion by 2025.

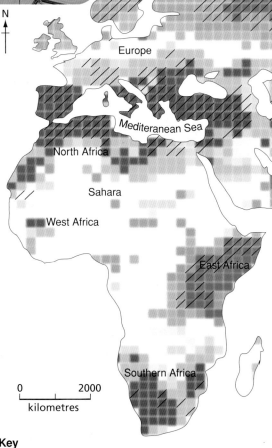

Key

percentage decrease (red) or increase (blue) in run-off as a result of changes to precipitation

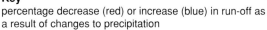
% −40 −20 −10 −5 −2 2 5 10 20 40

White areas are where different computer simulations are contradictory so no firm predictions can be made. Hatched areas are where different computer simulations are all in agreement.

Figure 25 Future patterns of run-off in Europe and Africa in 2090–99 (compared with 1990–99)

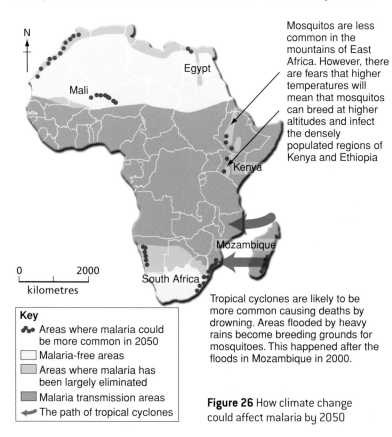

Mosquitos are less common in the mountains of East Africa. However, there are fears that higher temperatures will mean that mosquitos can breed at higher altitudes and infect the densely populated regions of Kenya and Ethiopia

Key
- 🦟 Areas where malaria could be more common in 2050
- ☐ Malaria-free areas
- ☐ Areas where malaria has been largely eliminated
- ☐ Malaria transmission areas
- ← The path of tropical cyclones

Tropical cyclones are likely to be more common causing deaths by drowning. Areas flooded by heavy rains become breeding grounds for mosquitoes. This happened after the floods in Mozambique in 2000.

Figure 26 How climate change could affect malaria by 2050

Activity

1 Use Figure 25 to describe the distribution of countries which are expected in the future to have:
   a) much less run-off
   b) much more run-off.

2 a) Explain how increased run-off might have positive and negative effects for people.
   b) Suggest why African countries might find it harder to cope with changes to run-off than European countries.

3 a) Use Figure 26 to describe the zone of Africa which is currently at risk from malaria.
   b) Describe how and why this zone is likely to change by 2050.

Mali   Climate change in Mali

Mali is a large country in West Africa situated immediately to the south of the Sahara desert. It is one of the poorest countries in the world. Rainfall is low and all regions of the country experience a long dry season. Since the 1960s annual rainfall totals have been much lower than in the earlier part of the twentieth century. Some regions of the country have less natural vegetation than 40 years ago so when it is windy the dry soil is easily blown away. This environmental problem is known as **desertification**.

Computer models suggest that rainfall in the region will continue to decline and that periods of drought will become more common. They also suggest that temperatures will be between 1.5 and 2.5 Celsius hotter by 2030. How will this affect the country and its people? Scientists believe that by 2030:

- cereal production will fall by 12 per cent
- cotton production will increase by 8 per cent
- livestock will have less food. Their weight when slaughtered will be 14–16 per cent lower than at present
- the percentage of population at risk of hunger will rise from 34 per cent to between 64 and 72 per cent.

Figure 27 Cotton is Mali's biggest export. Most is grown on a small scale by farmers who earn less than US$2 a day

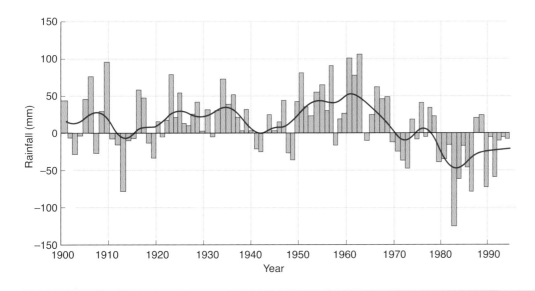

Figure 28 Annual rainfall anomalies in Sahel countries 1900–95. Each bar represents whether the total rainfall in each year was above or below average. The line shows the trend

Activity

4 Use Figure 28.
  a) How many years between 1900 and 1965 had:
    i) above average rainfall of 50 mm or more?
    ii) below average rainfall of –50 mm or less?
  b) How many years between 1965 and 2000 had:
    i) above average rainfall of 50 mm or more?
    ii) below average rainfall of –50 mm or less?

  c) Using evidence from Figure 28 compare rainfall patterns in the Sahel before 1965 with the period 1965–2000.

5 Outline the main climate change impacts on Mali using the following headings:
   Economy   Health   Water supply

Geography Futures

How can we create an alternative, low carbon future?

World leaders met in Kyoto, Japan to try to agree on how to tackle climate change. Many developed nations agreed to reduce their emission of greenhouse gases by five per cent below the levels they were emitting in 1990. This agreement is called the **Kyoto Protocol**.

However, the Kyoto Protocol is only a small step towards a low carbon future. While countries like the UK try to cut emissions, the growing economies of India and China are increasing their emissions. They argue that they need to increase electrical production to create wealth and get rid of poverty. So carbon dioxide levels (currently at around 380 ppm) are likely to increase for some years, even if European and other countries reduce their emissions. In 2008 the members of the EU agreed two new targets:

- to reduce overall CO_2 emissions by 20 per cent of their 1990 levels by the year 2020. This would be achieved by investment in renewable energy production using wind, solar and hydro-electricity.
- for each state to source at least 10 per cent of its transport fuel from **biofuel**. Biofuel is the kind of fuel that is made from natural plant oils. It is considered to be **carbon neutral** because these quick growing crops absorb as much carbon from the atmosphere while they are growing as they give off when they are burnt as fuel.

Activity

1 Create an advert or poster for biofuels that explains how they are carbon neutral.

2 a) Use Figure 28 to explain why the EU is keen to set much higher targets for carbon emission reductions than the Kyoto Protocol.

b) At what point do you think India and China should start reducing their emissions?

Model	Peak CO_2 level ppm	Year peak CO_2 is reached year	Change in CO_2 emissions in 2050 compared with 2000 per cent	Global average temperature increase compared with pre-industrial age Celsius	Global average sea level rise due to expansion of sea water but not taking ice melting into account metres
1	350–400	2000–2015	−85 – −50	2.0–2.4	0.4–1.4
2	400–440	2000–2020	−60 – −30	2.4–2.8	0.5–1.7
3	440–485	2010–2030	−30 – +5	2.8–3.2	0.6–1.9
4	485–570	2020–2060	+10 – +60	3.2–4.0	0.6–2.4
5	570–660	2050–2080	+25 – +85	4.0–4.9	0.8–2.9
6	660–790	2060–2090	+90 – +140	4.9–6.1	1.0–3.7

Figure 29 Computer models from the Intergovernmental Panel on Climate Change (IPCC), a highly respected group of climate scientists. Their computer models show that temperatures will rise even if we are able to control CO_2 concentrations below 400 ppm in the next five or so years. Model 1 would require the biggest and quickest cuts in CO_2 emissions, while model 6 allows countries to make smaller, slower cuts

Can new renewable technologies help us achieve a low carbon future?

Figure 30 may be a glimpse of a future, low carbon Europe. A field of 600 steel mirrors reflects solar energy. They direct a beam of light and heat to the top of a 40 m tower where the energy is focused on to water pipes. The heat turns the water to steam which then turns a turbine to generate electricity. The whole system is computer controlled so that each mirror tilts at exactly the right angle. At the moment this **solar furnace** produces enough energy for 6,000 homes, but the plant is being extended and will eventually provide power for the whole of the city of Seville, Spain.

In the future it would be possible to build more solar furnaces in the Sahara desert and bring their electricity into Europe through a new 'super-grid' of cables. Scientists believe that all of Europe's electricity could be generated from just 0.3 per cent of the sunlight that falls on the Sahara. The cost of the super-grid alone would be around €45 billion. This would certainly reduce Europe's carbon emissions dramatically, but critics point out that Africa should also benefit from some of this clean energy.

Figure 30 The new solar furnace which provides electricity for the city of Seville, Spain

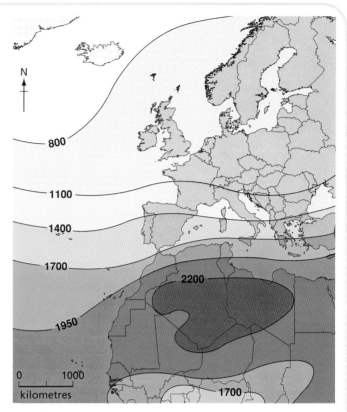

Figure 31 Patterns of solar energy across Europe and Africa. (kilowatts/m²/year)

Activity

3 Use Figure 31 to describe the distribution of countries that have:
   a) between 1,100 and 1,400 kilowatts/m²/year
   b) more than 2,200 kilowatts/m²/year.

4 Use Figure 32 to describe the distribution of:
   a) countries currently producing more than 2,000 megawatts of wind energy a year
   b) countries that could use their seas to make high levels of wave power.

5 Make a poster about renewable energy in Europe. Focus on wind, wave and solar. Include facts and figures about how much renewable energy is made in at least one European country.

Figure 32 In the future an international grid of power cables could link the countries of Europe and North Africa so that renewable energy made in the Sahara could be fed into your home

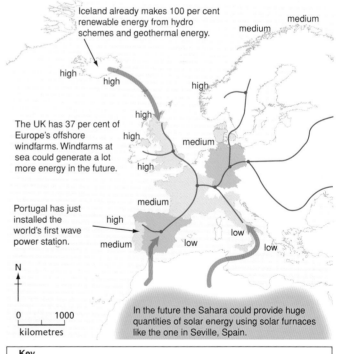

Iceland already makes 100 per cent renewable energy from hydro schemes and geothermal energy.

The UK has 37 per cent of Europe's offshore windfarms. Windfarms at sea could generate a lot more energy in the future.

Portugal has just installed the world's first wave power station.

In the future the Sahara could provide huge quantities of solar energy using solar furnaces like the one in Seville, Spain.

Key

☐ Countries already producing more than 10,000 mega watts of electricity from wind energy. One mega watt of wind energy is enough energy for around 300 homes.

☐ Countries already producing 2,000–4,000 mega watts of electricity from wind energy.

☐ high Areas of sea where wave power could be used to generate electricity.

Geography Futures

Attitudes to a low carbon future in the UK

A low carbon future could be achieved by combining three approaches.

- Using new technologies to reduce our dependence on fossil fuels for energy and transport.
- Better energy conservation and efficiency. This means changing our lifestyles so that each of us plays a part in reducing carbon emissions. For example, individuals can reduce energy consumption by insulating their homes, using low energy appliances, using more public transport and taking fewer flights.
- Finding ways to remove carbon dioxide from the atmosphere and storing it in long-term sinks such as forests or in rocks underground.

Each of these approaches to the low carbon future has advantages and disadvantages, and some may prove more popular than others. Figure 33 examines some different points of view on these low carbon solutions.

Figure 33 Different attitudes towards a low carbon future

Energy conservation and efficiency

Liberal Democrat politician

> My husband has a low-paid job and I work part time. We don't have much money. I'm worried we don't have enough money to put the heating on this winter. The TV news calls this fuel poverty. Our house was built in the 1930s and it doesn't have much insulation. I know that it would be good to insulate the roof. It would cost a bit less to heat the house and eventually the savings I make would pay for the work. But, you see, I really have no money to spare. The insulation will just have to wait.

> Everyone should do their bit to help save energy. Simple things like insulating the roof and only boiling as much water as you need every time you use the kettle. We estimate that the CO_2 emissions from electrical items left on standby in the UK is the same as 1.4 million long-haul flights. That's the same as everyone in Glasgow flying to New York and back! And the number of TVs is growing fast. We think that by 2020 there will be 74 million TVs in the UK, that's more TVs than people!

Young family

> We could capture carbon dioxide emissions from coal- and gas-fired power stations. The gas could then be turned to a liquid, pumped down into the ground and stored in sedimentary rocks. In fact, North Sea oil rigs that currently pump oil out of the ground could pump the CO_2 into the rocks when the oil has run out. Those rocks would make a perfect long-term carbon sink.
>
> The process is not difficult but would be quite expensive to set up. Each person in the UK makes about 10 tonnes of CO_2 each year by their use of energy. We estimate that the cost for capture and storage of CO_2 in North Sea rocks is about £20 per tonne. So it will cost about £200 per person each year. Would people want to pay?
>
> The government will have to find a way to make the power companies start to do this. The electricity generators have to capture the CO_2 and then transport it to a disposal site. The oil exploration companies will need to pay for the CO_2 to be stored deep underground. The government could threaten to tax these companies more unless they begin to capture and store the carbon.

Carbon capture and storage

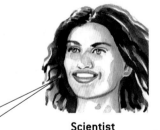

Scientist

Nuclear power or renewables?

Spokesperson for Friends of the Earth

> Some argue that nuclear power is a solution to climate change because it has no carbon emissions. But here at Friends of the Earth we oppose the building of any new nuclear power stations in the UK. We believe that nuclear power is dangerous for a number of reasons. Firstly, there is a security issue and power stations could be targets for terrorists. Secondly, there is the hazardous radioactive waste that will need careful management for generations. Finally, nuclear waste can be converted to be used in weapons.
>
> We are in favour of green energy which is energy from renewables such as wind and solar. These technologies are a safer, cheaper and cleaner solution to the problem of climate change.

Biofuels

There are a number of crops that produce oil that can be processed to make fuel for either cars or aircraft. The growth of these biofuels could reduce poverty in developing countries by creating jobs and wealth for farmers. At the same time people in the developed nations can continue to use their cars and take flights without the fear of oil shortages.

Industry spokesperson

Biofuel crops are causing poverty and hunger in some developing countries. Farmers are being encouraged to grow biofuels instead of food so that we can drive our cars without feeling guilty about carbon emissions. But here at Oxfam we believe that in 2007 and 2008 this has been a factor in the rising cost of food. Using the World Bank's figures we reckon that rising food prices have pushed 100 million people worldwide below the poverty line.

Since April 2008, all petrol and diesel in Britain has had to include 2.5 per cent from biofuels. The European Union considered raising that target to 10 per cent by 2020. However it is now concerned that this could push food prices even higher.

Spokesperson for Oxfam

Forest sinks

Spokesperson for Greenpeace

Planting trees seems like a really a good solution to climate change. They soak up carbon from the atmosphere and store it. However, here at Greenpeace we don't think that planting trees is enough. People have got to actually reduce their carbon emissions in order to tackle climate change. So planting a tree to offset your emissions is just not good enough.

We have been raising awareness of some companies who plant trees to offset their carbon emissions. For example, there is a Japanese power company who wanted to offset their carbon emissions by planting trees. So they bought some land in Tasmania, Australia. They cut down the natural forest that was growing here so they could plant 3,000 hectares of fast growing eucalyptus trees to soak up the carbon. How crazy is that!

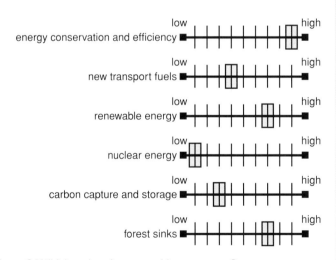

Figure 34 Which carbon future would you support?

Activity

1   Discuss the points of view shown in Figure 33. Outline some advantages and disadvantages of:
    a) energy efficiency and conservation
    b) biofuels
    c) nuclear power.

2   Explain why some environmentalists argue that planting forests is not a good enough option.

3   Working in pairs, study Figure 34.
    a) Imagine each slider represents the amount of effort and investment that could be made in the six possible solutions to climate change. Agree with your partner how each slider should be placed in your ideal low carbon future. Be prepared to justify your decision.
    b) Team up with another pair. Each pair must give a short presentation to describe and justify their low carbon future. Can you persuade the other pair to change their minds?

Changing our urban lifestyles

Climate change could have serious effects in large cities where heatwaves could become much more common. During heatwaves there are more days when people suffer from the uncomfortable effects of heat stress. In severe conditions, heatwaves can cause death, especially in the very young and very old. During the heatwave of August 2003, the temperature in central London was 9 °C higher than the surrounding countryside. Paris too was exceptionally hot and the extreme conditions caused at least 14,000 deaths in France.

The buildings and traffic in a large city influence the local climate, an effect known as **urban micro-climate**. One of the main impacts that a city has on the local climate is to create temperatures that are warmer than in the surrounding rural area. This is known as the **urban heat island.** The city acts like a massive storage heater, transferring heat from buildings and cars to the dome of air that covers the city.

- During the day, concrete, brick and tarmac absorb heat from the sun. This heat is then radiated into the atmosphere during the evening and at night.
- Buildings that are badly insulated lose heat energy, especially through roofs and windows. Heat is also created in cars and factories and this heat is also lost to the air from exhausts and chimneys.

Scientists know that the combination of climate change and the urban heat island are causing stress in some cities in the northern hemisphere. Figure 36 provides evidence of rising heat island effects in New York, Paris and Tokyo.

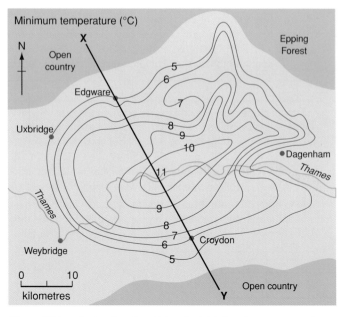

Figure 35 London's urban heat island, night-time temperatures in mid-May

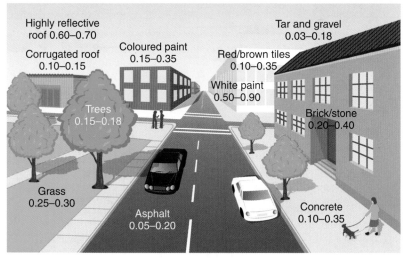

Figure 36 How the urban environment reflects the sun's energy. The closer the number to 1.0 the more energy is reflected. Surfaces with very low numbers are absorbing more of the sun's energy. They then emit this heat at night

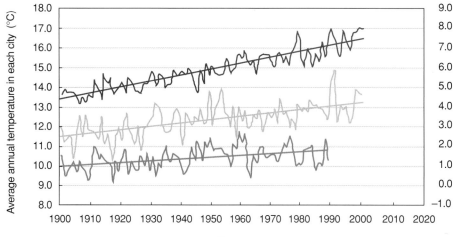

Figure 37 Trends in average urban temperatures in Tokyo, New York and Paris

What can be done about the urban heat island?

As temperatures rise more people install air-conditioning in their homes, but air-conditioning uses a lot of electrical energy. The production of more electricity creates the greenhouse gases that are causing climate change. It is estimated that the use of an air-conditioner for just one year in a hot climate such as Florida produces more CO_2 than a person in Cambodia produces in a lifetime. Figure 38 examines how the impact of the urban heat island could be reduced in the future.

> We need to reduce energy use. All new buildings must be well insulated to reduce heat loss. We need to design cars and air-conditioning that use less energy and have low emissions of greenhouse gases.

Engineer

Scientist

> We should create a network of parks so that the wind can blow through our cities and remove some of the heat. Cold groundwater can be pumped through pipes in our underground train stations. That would cool the air. The roofs of buildings can be coated in light-coloured materials to reflect sunshine.

> We need more green spaces. Parks reflect more of the sun's energy. More trees must be planted. The shade from trees reduces air temperatures. Trees soak up carbon dioxide and pollution from traffic.

Urban planner

Politician

> People need to change their lifestyles. People should take long holidays away from the city in the summer. We need to cut traffic by encouraging car users to switch to public transport. We can do this by congestion charging, as in Central London.

Figure 38 Possible ways of reducing the urban heat island

Activity

1 Use Figure 35.
   a) Describe the location of the area of highest temperatures in London.
   b) Describe the distribution of places with lower temperatures.
   c) Suggest reasons for the pattern shown on the map.

2 Use Figure 35 to draw a cross section of London's urban heat island along the line *x–y*.

3 a) Use Figure 36 to compare the urban heat island in each city.
   b) Use the trend to predict the urban heat island in each city by 2020.

4 Use Figures 37 and 38 to explain how the creation of more parks, woodlands and lakes in our cities might:
   a) affect the urban micro-climate
   b) make urban areas more sustainable in the future.

5 Use Figure 38 to outline the arguments for and against each of the following:

Strategy to reduce the urban heat island	Arguments for	Arguments against	Who might oppose this plan
Create more green spaces			
Reduce number of cars			
Design better homes			

Creating a sustainable future

The BedZed community is a **sustainable community** of 82 homes built in Beddington, Surrey. The homes are very energy efficient. The development only uses renewable energy sources: solar energy and wood chips. The development is claimed to be carbon neutral, in other words, the homes do not add any extra carbon dioxide emissions to the atmosphere. The government wants more carbon neutral schemes to be built. In fact, the government says 3 million new homes will be needed in the UK by 2020. How many will help create a low carbon future?

Activity

1 Discuss the features in Figures 39 and 40. Use this and the eco-schools website to audit (list the good and bad features) your own school. How could your community be more sustainable?

The buildings have 300 mm of insulation in the walls (most modern houses have 50 mm). This conserves heat energy so well that the homes need to be kept cool. These funnels direct fresh cool air into the buildings.

Large windows on the south side of the building collect heat energy from the sun – a technique known as passive solar gain.

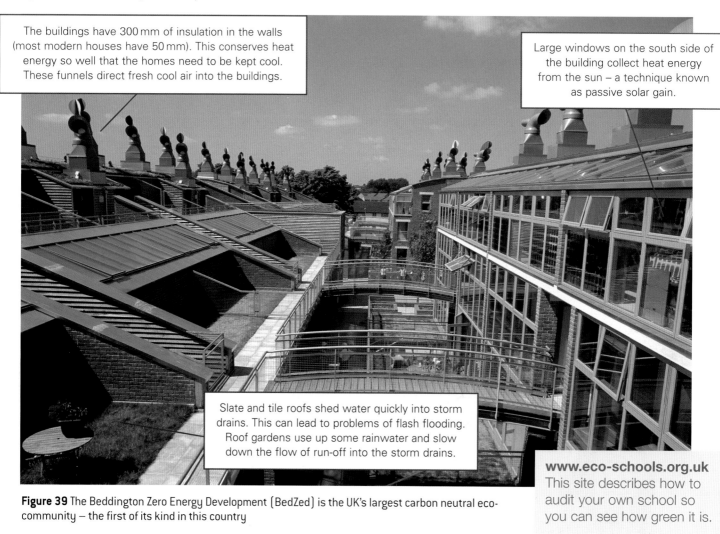

Slate and tile roofs shed water quickly into storm drains. This can lead to problems of flash flooding. Roof gardens use up some rainwater and slow down the flow of run-off into the storm drains.

www.eco-schools.org.uk
This site describes how to audit your own school so you can see how green it is.

Figure 39 The Beddington Zero Energy Development (BedZed) is the UK's largest carbon neutral eco-community – the first of its kind in this country

some affordable housing for people on lower incomes

a brownfield site rather than a greenfield site

jobs available locally

public transport available to everyone

A sustainable community has …

some buildings designed for elderly or disabled people with wide doorways for wheelchair users and ground-floor bedrooms and bathrooms

local facilities for people of all ages, e.g. crèche, youth group, community centre

green technologies to reduce heating costs and carbon emissions

schemes to reduce car ownership such as increased parking costs

Figure 40 Possible features of a sustainable community

Why are plate margins hazardous?

The ground beneath our feet is constantly on the move, although most of the time we are completely unaware of it. Occasionally, we get reminders of these forces in the form of earthquakes and volcanoes.

Who do you think visits this place and why?

How could this landscape have been created?

If the people crossed the footbridge would they be in a different continent? Why?

Why might this be a hazardous place to visit?

Figure 1 Thingvellir rift valley in Iceland

Activity

1 Look at Figure 1.
   a) Pick four words from the box below that best describe the photo.
   b) Discuss with a partner why you chose those words.
   c) Write a detailed justification why you feel the words describe the picture. What evidence is there to back up your explanation?

sparsely populated	poor natural resources	urban
managed	poor	tropical
good natural resources	rural	densely populated
wealthy	Arctic	safe
touristy	hazardous	remote

The **crust** is similar to the shell of a cracked egg. It is brittle and made up of large **plates** of rock. Underneath, the **mantle** is made up of molten rock. Temperatures here can vary greatly depending on the depth, with the hottest temperatures found near to the Earth's core. Hotter material rises towards the Earth's surface, where it cools and sinks back towards the core. These processes are known as convection currents. Over hundreds of millions of years, the plates, sitting on top of the mantle, have slowly been moving due to the convection currents. They move at an average speed of 2.5 cm per year.

What are plate margins?

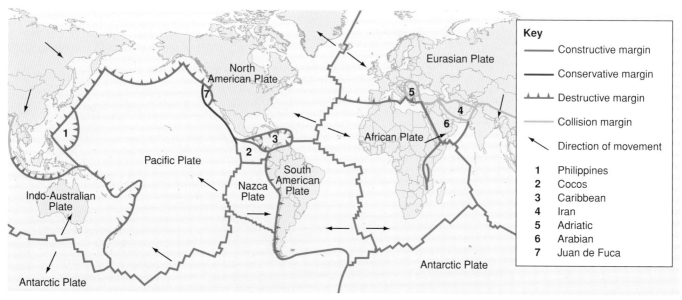

Figure 2 Plate margins and the direction of movement

Plate margins produce distinct and dramatic landforms as well as posing various hazards to the people who live in these areas. Some plates are moving towards each other (**destructive plate margin**) and others are moving away from each other (**constructive plate margin**).

What happens at constructive plate margins?

At constructive plate margins, two plates are pulling apart. Below the Earth's surface, magma wells up, cools and fills the gap between the plates, forming new crust material. Where this occurs under the sea, the continuous action of plates pulling apart and forming new oceanic crust results in a clearly defined **oceanic ridge**. This is occurring in the middle of the Atlantic Ocean. The Mid-Atlantic Ridge is evidence that the Eurasian Plate is moving away from the

North American Plate as can be seen in Figure 3. Because the pulling apart of the plates is not uniform along the length of the margin, large fracture zones occur along the ridge. So rather than the ridge forming a straight line it is offset by the fractures. As the plates move apart, friction increases in the fractures. When the pressure becomes too great there is a sudden release of energy, much like an elastic band snapping, and there is an earthquake. Most earthquakes occurring at this type of plate margin are shallow as the point of friction is relatively close to the surface in the crust.

Activity

1 Find Iceland on Figure 2.
   a) Describe Iceland's location.
   b) Knowing Iceland's location, how could you alter your choice of words to describe Figure 1?

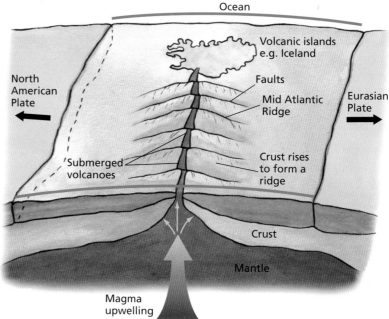

Figure 3 Landforms of a constructive plate margin

Iceland

Constructive plate margins not only occur beneath the sea but on land too. Much of Iceland's unique landscape is due to the fact that it sits astride the Mid-Atlantic Ridge. Iceland is actually being gradually torn in two and this is evident at Thingvellir as shown in Figure 4. Over time, a giant fissure 7.7 km long has opened in the Earth's surface. As it has widened, the land at the centre of the fissure has sunk down forming a **rift valley** with steep, escarpments running along both sides.

This area is volcanic as magma is very close to the Earth's surface. Typically volcanoes at constructive plate margins are some of the largest volcanoes in the world in terms of their area. Lava here has a low viscosity, i.e. it is very runny and so flows over a wide area. Icelandic people termed these **shield volcanoes** because of their low, broad appearance similar to a warrior's shield. Ash released from these volcanoes tends to build up around vents forming a steep, round hill known as a **cinder cone**.

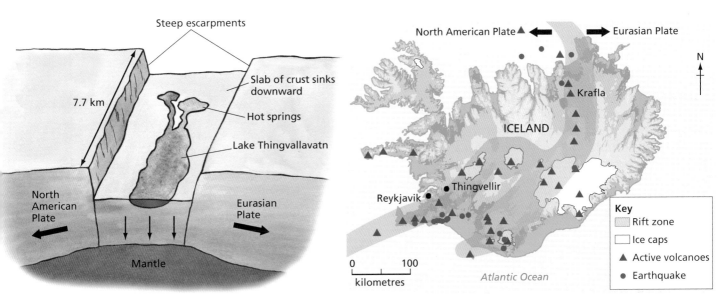

Figure 4 Formation of the rift valley at Thingvellir

Figure 5 Map of Iceland showing where the Mid-Atlantic Ridge crosses the country

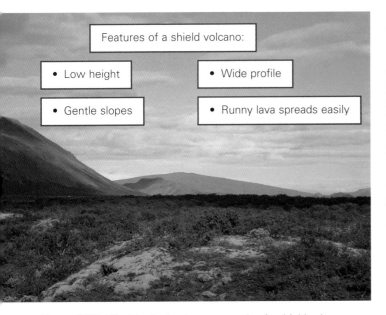

Features of a shield volcano:
- Low height
- Wide profile
- Gentle slopes
- Runny lava spreads easily

Figure 6 Skjaldbreidur, Iceland – an example of a shield volcano

Activity

2 Study Figures 1 and 4. Make a brief sketch of Thingvellir with annotations of the landforms and processes.

3 Why are the springs at Thingvellir hot?

4 Using Figures 3 and 4, explain how Iceland's physical geography could change over the next million years.

5 Study Figure 5.
   a) Come up with a hypothesis about the distribution of volcanoes and earthquakes in Iceland.
   b) Produce a brief report describing the distribution using evidence to support your hypothesis.

What happens at destructive plate margins?

A destructive plate margin is an area where two plates are moving towards each other. There are two types: continental crust colliding with oceanic crust, and oceanic crust colliding with oceanic crust. The point where the two plates meet is known as the **subduction zone** where one plate is forced down under the other into the mantle. The subducted plate is cooler and denser than the surrounding mantle and gravity pulls it down. This process, known as slab pull, is thought to be responsible for continental drift.

Along the coast of South America, the Nazca Plate is moving towards the South American plate. The Nazca Plate being oceanic and therefore denser, is subducted underneath the continental crust into the mantle, as shown in Figure 7. As the Nazca Plate bends down into the mantle it forms a deep **oceanic trench** 5,900 km long and over 8,000 metres deep in places.

The force of one plate being dragged under another causes intense friction and the pressure increases. Eventually, the pressure becomes too great and the two plates will move in a sudden jolt, causing an earthquake. Where an oceanic plate meets a continental plate, sediments are thrust upwards. Because of the intense friction caused by the plates scraping against each other, the temperature in the mantle increases. Magma rises forming a long chain of volcanic **fold mountains** (e.g. the Andes).

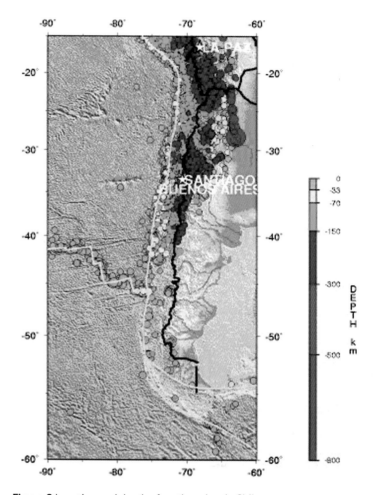

Figure 8 Location and depth of earthquakes in Chile

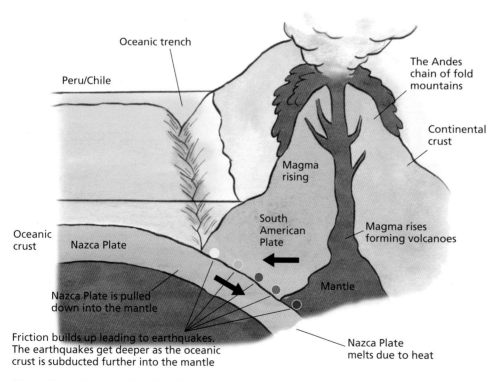

Figure 7 Landforms produced at a destructive plate margin – subduction of the Nazca Plate

Where two oceanic plates move towards each other, one plate is subducted under the other. This occurs in the Caribbean where the North American Plate is being subducted under the Caribbean plate as shown in Figure 9. Again, an oceanic trench is formed. As the North American Plate is subducted it drags down sediment and water from the sea bed. This mixture melts into the mantle due to the friction and heat. The increase in heat causes magma to rise upwards into the Caribbean crust, which in turn forms a chain of volcanic islands, known as an **island arc.** The island of Montserrat is part of the West Indies island arc. The Soufriere Hills volcano on the island has been erupting since 1995 after lying dormant for over 300 years. It is an example of a **strato-volcano** that has been built up over time from layers of ash, lava and other volcanic debris.

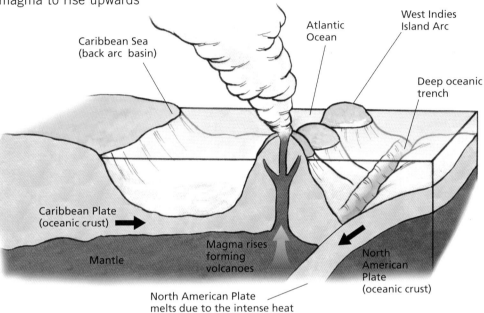

Figure 9 Landforms at a destructive plate margin where ocean crust is subducted beneath ocean crust as it is in the Caribbean region

Features of a strato-volcano:

• steep gradients

• layers of ash and lava

• high summit

• explosive eruptions

Figure 10 A strato-volcano

Activity

1 Describe how plates move.

2 Draw a table like the one shown below. List the landforms occurring at each plate margin giving a brief description of each.

Constructive plate margin	Destructive plate margin

3 How do volcanoes differ at constructive plate margins and at destructive plate margins?

4 Use Figures 7 and 8.
   a) Describe the pattern of earthquakes at a destructive plate margin.
   b) Give reasons for the pattern. How might this be different from a constructive plate margin?

What are the primary and secondary hazards of volcanic eruptions?

The hazards associated with volcano and earthquake zones can be separated into two categories.

- **Primary hazards** are those that occur as a direct result of the earthquake or volcanic eruption.
- **Secondary hazards** are those that occur because of a change in the environment following an earthquake or eruption.

One of the most common and particularly dangerous volcanic hazards is a **pyroclastic flow.** Huge burning clouds (at temperatures up to 1000 °C) of ash, gas and **tephra** are blasted into the air. This material is very dense and it races down the volcano's slopes at speeds of 200 km/hr. Vegetation is scorched and trees are uprooted by the intense force of the cloud. In Iceland, pyroclastic flows are extremely rare. They are more common on destructive plate margins, where the lava is thicker and more explosive – for example on the Caribbean island of Montserrat.

Another common and dangerous hazard are **lahars** or mudflows. Glacial meltwater and heavy rains falling on volcanic slopes act as triggers for these flows. Water mixes with ash and other debris creating a cement-like flow. They travel at great speed covering tens of kilometres, leaving a path of destruction in their wake.

Figure 11 A pyroclastic flow surges down the slopes of the Soufriere Hills volcano in Montserrat

Grimsvötn, Iceland Case study of the eruption of Grimsvötn, Iceland

Iceland is particularly vulnerable as it experiences frequent earthquakes and volcanic events. Adding to the hazards, many of the volcanoes are situated under ice caps, which cover 11 per cent of the country. Grimsvötn is Iceland's most active volcano of recent times.

Figure 12 Location of Grimsvötn

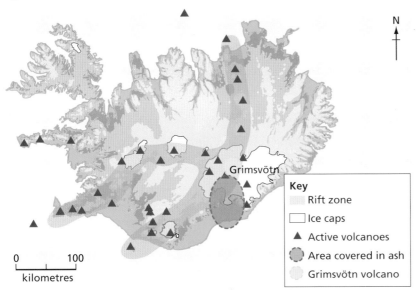

Key
Rift zone
Ice caps
Active volcanoes
Area covered in ash
Grimsvötn volcano

Throughout the Grimsvötn eruptions huge clouds of **ash** were released high into the atmosphere causing disruption to air traffic across Europe. One plume spread as far as Norway and Finland.

Sometimes areas near to volcanoes suffer from ash falls, just like heavy rain. The weight of ash deposits on buildings can cause roofs to collapse. Ash can contaminate water supplies and smother crops. In 1783, the Laki volcano in Iceland was responsible for causing the deaths of over 200,000 livestock because they ate grass contaminated with ash. In the famine that followed more than 10,000 people died. More than 15 km^2 of lava flowed over the land and ash blocked sunlight for two years and altered temperatures.

Lava flows were recorded in the 1996 eruption although these took place under the ice cap. Most Icelandic volcanoes produce lava that has a low viscosity (runny) and so can spread over a large area when eruptions take place in the open air. Lava flows are not usually life threatening as they move relatively slowly. However, buildings, roads and trees in the flow's path will be destroyed.

Fact file
- Iceland's most active volcano
- Under Vatnajökull ice cap
- 200 m thick ice above caldera lake
- Recently erupted 1996, 1998, 2004
- Subglacial lake empties every 5–10 years

Figure 13 Grimsvötn erupting from beneath the Vatnajökull ice cap

51

Figure 14 A jökulhaup that occurred following the eruption of Grimsvötn in 1996

The 1996 eruption was particularly dramatic, producing many primary and secondary effects (Figure 14). The eruption continued for six weeks. During this time, the base of the ice melted forming a **subglacial** lake, which filled the **caldera**. Eventually 3 km² of water had collected, enough to lift the ice cap. On 4 November 1996, 50 km from the volcano, the meltwater burst out from under the glacier in a surging torrent. The flood, known as a **jökulhaup,** carried huge icebergs and sediment with it. It destroyed several bridges and washed away part of the Iceland ring road. Due to the isolated location, luckily no lives were lost.

Activity

1 Why is Iceland particularly at risk from jökulhaups?

2 Look at Figure 15. Copy and complete the table below sorting out the primary and secondary hazards associated with volcanoes. Give a brief description of each.

Primary hazards	Secondary hazards

3 Suggest what would happen if an event similar to the 1783 eruption took place now. Would it be as devastating?

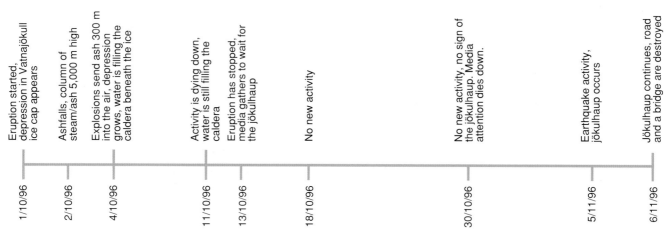

Figure 15 Timeline of 1996 Grimsvötn eruption events

Eruption started, depression in Vatnajökull ice cap appears — 1/10/96

Ashfalls, column of steam/ash 5,000 m high — 2/10/96

Explosions send ash 300 m into the air, depression grows, water is filling the caldera beneath the ice — 4/10/96

Activity is dying down, water is still filling the caldera — 11/10/96

Eruption has stopped, media gathers to wait for the jökulhaup — 13/10/96

No new activity — 18/10/96

No new activity, no sign of the jökulhaup. Media attention dies down. — 30/10/96

Earthquake activity, jökulhaup occurs — 5/11/96

Jökulhaup continues, road and a bridge are destroyed — 6/11/96

GIS Activity: Iceland's hazard zones

http://gullhver.os.is/website/hpf/orkustofnun_english/viewer.htm

The weblink will take you to a digital atlas of Iceland. The base map shows faint blue lines for the coast and rivers. Tools on the left allow you to zoom in and out. Click on the dialogue boxes in the menu on the right to switch on various layers, which include features such as volcanoes and hot springs.

The heat of the rocks at Hengill is used in a number of ways. Local farmers use hot water from the ground to heat commercial greenhouses growing flowers, tomatoes and cucumbers. Steam is also piped from the ground at high pressure to generate power for the capital, Reykjavik. Tourists hike in the area to see the bubbling mud pools.

Hekla is an active volcano. It had a massive eruption in 1947. The mountain is a long thin ridge and fissure eruptions occur along this ridge roughly every 10 years.

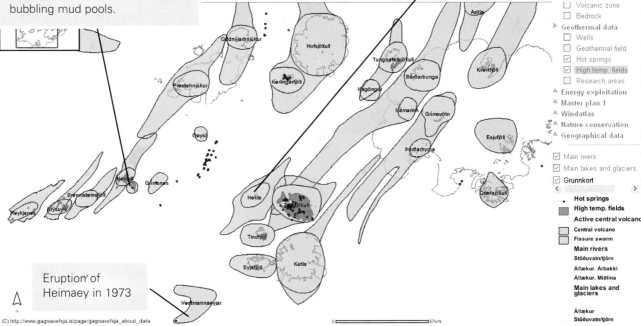

Eruption of Heimaey in 1973

Figure 16 Screenshot showing geothermal zones and active volcanoes in south-west Iceland

For more info on the rift valley in Iceland see **www.thingvellir.is/english/maps**

Activity

1 Use Figure 16 and the weblink above.
   a) Describe the location of Hekla.
   b) Use the photo and your understanding of constructive plate margins to describe five primary hazards associated with this kind of eruption.

2 a) Describe the distribution of hot springs on Figure 16.

   b) Describe the distribution of high temperature fields compared with active central volcanoes.
   c) Suggest reasons for these patterns.

3 Produce a 500-word report explaining three different benefits that Iceland's geology brings to its people.

What are the primary and secondary effects associated with earthquakes?

Earthquakes also produce both primary and secondary hazards. Primary hazards are those that occur as a direct result of an earthquake. An example of a secondary hazard would be a tsunami when there has been an earthquake under the ocean floor. The Asian tsunami of 26 December 2004 killed 230,000, proving how secondary hazards are often more devastating than the initial event.

| Sichuan, China | ### Case study of the Sichuan earthquake in China |

| Town of Beichuan was left in rubble after the earthquake. | Landslide triggered by earthquake | Lake formed behind the landslide | Engineers drained the 'quake lake' flooding the river valley below. |

Figure 17 Beichuan before and after the earthquake – landslides blocked rivers forming 'quake lakes'

The town of Beichuan was evacuated before the flood. It is to be rebuilt elsewhere.

On 12 May 2008, Sichuan province in south-west China was struck by a strong earthquake measuring 7.9 on the Richter scale.

Around 87,000 people lost their lives as buildings were reduced to rubble due to the intense ground shaking. Strong **aftershocks** (measuring up to 6.1 on the Richter scale) continued in the weeks after the event, causing further damage and hampering rescue efforts.

In Sichuan, the highest concentrations of people and buildings are found in the river valleys. When the marshy soil was violently shaken it lost its strength and became very soft – like wet concrete. This process is called **liquefaction.** The foundations of buildings were not supported and collapsed easily.

In the town of Beichuan, one of the worst hit areas, 80 per cent of buildings collapsed. Those who survived faced the prospect of secondary hazards.

The earthquake triggered a landslide blocking the Jian River. The water level rose quickly in the valley behind the dam, creating a 'quake lake'. (More than 30 of these were formed across Sichuan.) Aftershocks threatened to collapse these debris dams and send a torrent of water downstream. Beichuan was evacuated while engineers created channels to drain the water. Eventually, the water broke and flooded Beichuan and the valley downstream (Figure 17).

In built-up areas, fire can be a major threat in the immediate moments after an earthquake. Ruptured gas pipes ignite and fire can quickly spread amongst the rubble. Small fires burned in Sichuan but were quickly got under control. The earthquake derailed trains and landslides blocked roads, making it very difficult to get assistance to where it was needed. Industries shut down because many workers had been killed. Rice crops were either destroyed or had to be harvested early to make way for refugee camps that were needed to house the 4.8 million homeless people. Survivors faced an uncertain future.

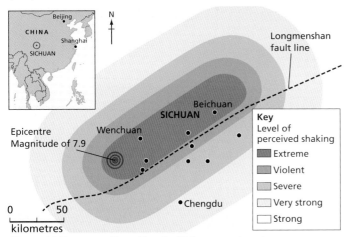

Figure 18 The area affected by the Sichuan earthquake

Power cables brought down

4.8 million people homeless

375,000 injured

How will this man drink and eat?

Powerful aftershocks continued for months

Where will this man find shelter?

Increased threat of diseases such as cholera and dysentery

Communication links destroyed

Figure 19 Earthquake damage in Sichuan province, China

Activity

1 Make a list of the primary and secondary hazards associated with earthquakes.

2 What were the effects of the Sichuan earthquake on:
   a) the economy
   b) the environment
   c) the people?

3 Study Figure 20.
   a) Create a hypothesis to explain the relationship between earthquake size and number of deaths.
   b) Plot a scattergraph for the data in Figure 20 using different colours for LEDCs and MEDCs. (Show the magnitude on the *x* axis and the death toll on the *y* axis.)
   c) Give a detailed explanation for the pattern shown in the graph.

4 Study the words in the box below.
   Evaluate the impact these factors may have on surviving earthquake hazards.

wealth	aid and relief
population density	corruption

Date	Location	Richter scale magnitude	Deaths
12.05.08	Sichuan, China	8.0	65,000
26.12.04	Sumatra, Indonesia	9.3	300,000
26.12.03	Bam, Iran	6.6	30,000
26.01.01	Gujarat, India	7.7	20,085
17.08.99	Izmit, Turkey	7.6	17,118
17.01.95	Japan	7.2	5,000
15.02.94	Indonesia	6.5	37
17.01.94	Los Angeles, US	6.6	57
30.09.93	India	6.4	22,000
12.07.93	Japan	7.8	26
12.12.92	Indonesia	6.8	1,912
28.06.92	California, US	7.4	1
25.04.92	California, US	6.9	0
13.03.92	Turkey	6.8	1,000
01.02.91	Afghanistan/ Pakistan border	6.8	1,200
16.07.90	Philippines	7.7	1,621
21.06.90	Iran	7.3–7.7	50,000

Figure 20 Major earthquakes 1972–2008

Why do people continue to live in hazard zones?

It is estimated that 500 million people, one twelfth of the world's population, live in active zones. The hazards are obvious, so there must be reasons why people continue to live in these areas. Most of the time, the majority of people are able to go about their daily business without worrying about the potential risks. Often many are unaware of the threats as incidents are rare but have high levels of disruption.

Figure 21 The Philippines is situated on a destructive plate margin. Most of the population is at risk from volcanic and earthquake hazards

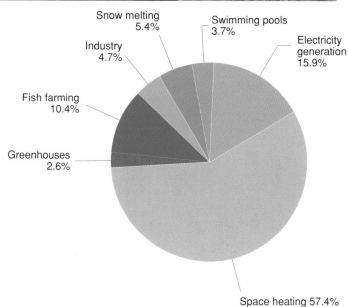

Figure 22 Iceland has many uses for geothermal energy

Iceland makes the most of its location in a volcanic zone. The country relies heavily on **geothermal energy**. Magma below the Earth's crust heats the rocks above. The heat is used to produce steam to drive turbines producing electricity. Left over heat is used locally to heat buildings. Geothermal energy is a **renewable** energy source. It is cheap to produce, readily available in Iceland and does not emit greenhouse gases. Today 18 per cent of the country's electricity comes from geothermal supplies. Figure 22 shows how geothermal energy is used.

Volcanoes are a natural attraction for curious tourists. Jobs are created and money comes into the local economy so local people benefit. Services and infrastructure are also improved to cater for the increased numbers of visitors. Tourists are drawn to the spectacular scenery, hot spas (Iceland) and ski resorts (Mount Etna, Italy). Specialist tour companies provide trips to remote volcanic areas. The island of Montserrat in the Caribbean had a thriving tourist industry prior to the eruption of the Soufriere Hills volcano in 1995. The volcano continues even today. Pyroclastic flows destroyed the original airport. Only half of the island is declared as safe. Since 1995 visitor numbers have steadily been increasing (Figure 23).

Ash from volcanoes is rich in nutrients. Over time, deposits build up providing fertile soils that are ideal for growing crops. For farmers, this benefit outweighs the hazards of living here.

In LEDCs, many people simply do not have the choice of moving away from hazard zones. Countries like the Philippines sit on one of the most active plate margins in the world. Strong earthquakes and volcanic eruptions are a frequent occurrence. The majority of the population lives in poor quality housing. When an incident occurs people living here are usually the hardest hit. The population experiences financial inertia; they are financially unable to move to safer areas even if they wanted to.

Year	Total Number of tourists
1994	36,267
1998	9,427
2002	9,623
2006	7,991

Figure 23 Number of tourists visiting Montserrat

Country of Residence	2002	2003	2004	2005	2006	2006 (%)
United States	1950	1541	2084	2034	2153	26.9
Canada	375	297	334	404	393	4.9
United Kingdom	2581	2269	3021	2968	2321	29.0
Other Europe	178	145	176	228	180	2.3
OECS*	3282	2849	3051	2297	1540	19.3
Other Caribbean	1171	1224	1334	1690	1328	16.6
Rest of World	86	65	138	69	76	1.0
TOTAL	**9623**	**8390**	**10138**	**9690**	**7991**	**100.0**

* OECS = Organisation of Eastern Caribbean States

Figure 24 Origin of visitors to Montserrat (2002–2006)

Activity

1 What is geothermal energy?

2 Explain the benefits of geothermal energy to Iceland, and mention some of its uses.

3 Study Figures 23 and 24.
   a) Draw a graph to show the trend in visitor numbers since 1994.
   b) Mark on the graph the July 1995 eruption.
   c) Explain what the graph shows.
   d) Use the data to describe and explain the origin of visitors to Montserrat.

   e) Discuss with the person next to you, which types of people would be most likely to visit Montserrat. Write down your ideas, giving reasons.

4 Do you think the benefits of living in a hazard zone outweigh the problems? Write approximately 200 words to justify your opinion.

How can the risks associated with volcanic and earthquake zones be reduced?

How are volcanoes monitored and what does this tell us about their state?

The world's active volcanoes are constantly monitored to try to predict when the next eruptive event will take place. Scientists are able to recognise certain signs. Particular attention is given to volcanoes close to large urban populations, e.g. Mount Etna, Italy.

Increased seismicity – frequent earthquakes

Increased heat given off

Sulphur dioxide and CO_2 released

Erosion of volcanic deposits

Ground **deformation** – change in shape

Figure 25 Scientists monitor volcanoes to try to predict when an eruption will take place

Soufriere Hills, Montserrat

The Soufriere Hills volcano in Montserrat has been erupting since 1995, giving scientists at the Montserrat Volcano Observatory (MVO) valuable opportunities for research. Although the volcano is active, it goes through periods of relative quiet but may suddenly become violent. In Figure 26 a volcanologist from MVO describes how monitoring the volcano gave clues to a recent explosive event.

'At MVO we use a number of techniques to keep a check on what the volcano's doing. Our observatory is situated three miles from the volcano so we have a clear view of it (when it's not hidden by cloud!) Before the eruptive event of 28 July 2008, the lava dome swelled in size, indicating magma was moving upwards in the volcano. The sides of the dome are made of loose material. As it grows, rockfalls are triggered. For the three weeks leading up to the 28 July, numbers of rockfalls had been slightly higher.

I'd been recording the number of earthquakes and noticed a significant increase in the week before the event. Thirty times as many earthquakes occurred in one week than in the whole of June! That's a sure sign something's going on. As the magma was moving up, the pressure inside the volcano grew causing cracks, which were experienced as small earthquakes. More pressure means more earthquakes.

A colleague of mine had recorded a steady increase in the amount of sulphur dioxide given off. This is a forewarning of an event as it implies that magma is moving closer to the surface.

Over the course of June and early July, there was little visible activity other than occasional ash plumes. It's only because of our scientific readings that we knew there was going to be an event. That's why our job is so important, we are able to give warnings and assist in planning hazard maps.'

Figure 26 A volcanologist from MVO describes monitoring the volcano

Activity

1 Look at Figure 25. One of the signs is an odd one out. Which one is it and why?
2 Copy and complete the following table using the information on these two pages.

Sign a volcano may erupt	What it tells us about the volcano
Change in shape of lava dome	
	Pressure is increasing inside the volcano…

3 Study the data in Figure 27.
   a) Draw a graph to show the results of SO_2 emissions.
   b) Draw a graph to show the number of rockfalls and earthquakes.
   c) Use full sentences. Describe the pattern of:
      i) SO_2 emissions
      ii) rockfalls and earthquakes.
   d) What is the percentage increase in SO_2 emissions between 31 May and the eruption?

Date w/c 2008	Activity	Average SO_2 tons/ day (t/d)	Earth-quakes	Rock-falls
31 May	low	206	20	9
07 June	low	228	14	17
14 June	low	254	14	2
21 June	low	323	6	6
28 June	low	329	5	0
05 July	low	339	10	10
11 July	low	414	8	13
21 July	increased	378	145	18
28 July	high	3000	1694	25

Figure 27 Data from MVO leading to a pyroclastic flow
Source: Montserrat Volcano Observatory

4 Suggest a hypothesis for the number of earthquakes and rockfalls in the build up to an eruption.

5 What other data could be included in the table to tell us about the state of the volcano?

6 Explain the difficulties of monitoring volcanoes.

How might the effects of volcanic eruptions and earthquakes be reduced in LEDCs and MEDCs?

Both LEDCs and MEDCs take short-term and long-term measures to minimise the impact of disasters. Usually, the effects of volcanoes and earthquakes have greatest impact on people living in LEDCs. Richer MEDCs have invested heavily in protecting themselves and their economies from disaster.

What is done in the short term to minimise the effects of volcanoes and earthquakes?

China In the aftermath of a volcanic eruption or earthquake, people are likely to be traumatised and may still be at risk of further hazards. A swift and targeted response is necessary to minimise the effects. Following the devastating Sichuan earthquake on 12 May 2008 (87,000 people lost their lives) the Chinese government responded quickly and deployed over 50,000 army troops to assist with the relief effort.

Figure 28 China responded quickly to the disaster

In the first few days, rescuers had to sift through rubble by hand to get to trapped survivors. Heavy earth-moving equipment was needed although the scale of the disaster meant that China had to ask for assistance from the international community. Small teams from Japan, experts in earthquake rescue, were sent to Sichuan. Six weeks after the disaster, the Chinese government had organised the evacuation of nearly 1.47 million people from the worst affected areas. Temporary camps were set up to provide survivors with shelter; 34,000 tents were used. It became a race against time to provide the huge numbers of survivors with clean drinking water, shelter, food and medical supplies. Some towns such as Beichuan, where 80 per cent of the buildings were destroyed are to be rebuilt elsewhere.

The towns and villages on the flanks of Mount Etna in Italy are regularly under threat from lava flows. Diverting lava flows is a costly option. Efforts in the seventeenth century to control the lava flow resulted in laws banning the practice on the slopes of Etna. To protect one village usually meant sacrificing another. These laws were scrapped in 1983 and authorities now try several methods to divert flows.

Some of the more successful methods used around the world have been:

- spraying lava with water – this cools it and solidifies it
- earth barriers to channel the direction of the lava flow
- dropping concrete blocks via helicopter to divert the flow
- aerial bombing lava tubes with dynamite to widen them and dissipate the flow.

Lava diversion can be controversial. From a practical point of view, lava diversion can only be used where the topographical conditions are favourable. When lava is diverted on to property that would have been spared there are complex legal issues. It also raises political and social issues. Should the authorities let nature take its course? Financially it is expensive. The Mauna Loa volcano observatory in Hawaii is protected by barriers as it was financially viable. For properties of a lower value it may not be worth the expense.

To reduce fatalities people are evacuated from risk areas. Repeatedly evacuating people can be expensive and disruptive for the evacuees. Longer term solutions are more favourable.

Activity

1 Make a list of the short-term measures taken to reduce volcano and earthquake hazards.
   a) Draw a Venn diagram like the one below.
   b) Insert the words from your list into the Venn diagram (LEDC/MEDC).

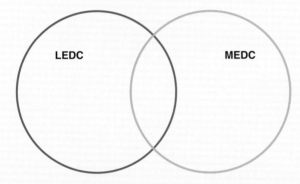

2 What are the advantages and disadvantages of controlling lava flows?

3 Look at the decision-making exercise on the right.
   a) Imagine you are the mayor of the town. Decide which of the options you would follow.
   b) Write a 250-word report justifying your decision.

Decision-making exercise on lava flow

Nicolosi is a small town on the flanks of Mount Etna in Italy with a population of around 6,500. Several times, lava has threatened the town, most recently in 2001. The authorities wonder how to tackle the problem.

Imagine you are the mayor of Nicolosi and a recent eruption has sent lava flowing down the slopes to once again threaten the town. How do you react?

Decide from the following options which course of action to take. Explain the reasons for your choice fully. What will the consequences of your decision be?

- Do nothing to the lava flow and evacuate the town (knowing you may have to evacuate again in the future).
- Attempt to divert the flow using concrete blocks. Taking this approach will mean sacrificing several properties outside the village.
- Evacuate the town and resettle inhabitants in a newly built town situated a safe distance from Mount Etna.
- Construct concrete defences around key buildings at risk.

What long-term measures are there to reduce the impact of volcanoes and earthquakes?

Long-term measures involve plans to prepare people and technology to reduce the risks associated with volcanoes and earthquakes. High risk areas such as California are prone to frequent earthquakes. A large earthquake there could be deadly and also extremely damaging to the economy. A lot of money has been invested in measures to reduce the risks.

LEDCs are often less prepared for earthquake and volcano disasters as there tends to be less financial investment in early warning systems. Across the Indian Ocean, following the devastating tsunami of 26 December 2004, a tsunami early warning system is now operational. The system provides warnings to people living in vulnerable areas, giving them time to get to higher ground. The financial investment for this scheme has come from countries around the Indian Ocean as well as from the wider international community.

Figure 29 Flyer for a 'Shake Out' event

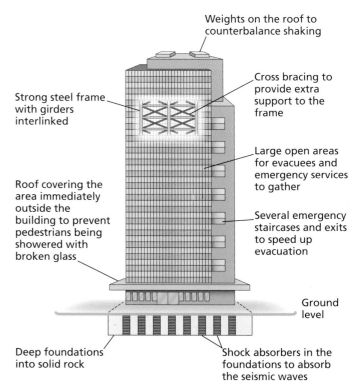

Weights on the roof to counterbalance shaking

Cross bracing to provide extra support to the frame

Strong steel frame with girders interlinked

Large open areas for evacuees and emergency services to gather

Roof covering the area immediately outside the building to prevent pedestrians being showered with broken glass

Several emergency staircases and exits to speed up evacuation

Ground level

Deep foundations into solid rock

Shock absorbers in the foundations to absorb the seismic waves

Figure 30 Earthquake proof building

Large urban areas in MEDCs rely on an emergency planning system. Emergency services are trained to deal with a volcanic eruption or earthquake. Specialist teams can be deployed immediately with equipment for locating survivors underneath rubble. Earthquake education and drills are even incorporated into the school curriculum in southern California. One worry is that people become complacent to the risk so events like the 'Shake Out' in California are held (Figure 29). The annual event aims to raise awareness of the risks of a major earthquake, so damage can be limited.

In earthquake areas, new buildings, roads and bridges are designed to withstand earthquakes and minimise any damage (Figure 30). Local planners also strictly control new developments, avoiding areas that may be too risky.

Activity

1 List the long-term measures to reduce volcano and earthquake hazards, giving a brief description of each.

2 Explain the differences between short-term and long-term measures to reduce volcano and earthquake hazards.

3 Suggest where volcanoes and earthquakes are likely to have most impact: LEDCs or MEDCs?

4 Compare how LEDCs and MEDCs reduce the impact of volcanoes and earthquakes.

How does technology help monitor volcanoes?

Scientists use a range of technological methods to monitor volcanoes. Since the eruption of the Soufriere Hills volcano started in 1995, the Montserrat Volcano Observatory (MVO) has improved the methods of data collection as new technologies are available.

Several monitoring stations are positioned around the volcano and are powered by a solar panel and a 12V battery. Much of the equipment can be operated remotely, only requiring routine maintenance from time to time. One of the most valuable tools is a seismograph. These record even the smallest tremors. Signals are sent back to the observatory where volcanologists interpret the results and issue warnings when the number of earthquakes increases.

Changes in the shape of the volcano (the deformation of it) are measured using several techniques. Global Positioning System (GPS) satellites record the exact position of every monitoring station. Although the satellites are in space, they can record the slightest change in shape of the volcano. A second method involves a laser beam being sent from one point on the volcano to another where a mirror is positioned. If there is the slightest change in ground shape this is recorded. **Tiltmeters** are also used although generally these only record large-scale movements.

Levels of sulphur dioxide are recorded from two to five times a week. This involves taking gas readings from locations around the volcano. Any work carried out on the slopes of the volcano can be dangerous.

Visual monitoring of the volcano is extremely important too, particularly for monitoring the growth of the lava dome. Remote cameras, set up around the volcano, take regular photographs. The MVO also flies over the Soufriere Hills to take aerial photographs when cloud cover permits. RADAR and remote sensing using satellites are also used. These provide quality images of the volcano regardless of the weather conditions.

Figure 31 Images of the dome of the Soufriere Hills Volcano, Montserrat, taken from the helicopter at an altitude of 4,000ft. The top image combines a photograph with a thermal image taken at the same time. Hot areas show up as warmer colours in the thermal image

Montserrat   Hazard mapping

Hazard mapping reduces the impact of a volcano or earthquake by limiting access or controlling development in certain zones. The southern part of Montserrat has been divided into six zones (Figures 32 and 33). A hazard level system is operated, restricting access to certain areas depending on how active the volcano is. Much of the island is out of bounds except to scientists. Daytime access to some areas is permitted. There are also maritime exclusion zones as some of the pyroclastic flows reach the coast. More than two thirds of the 11,500 population of Montserrat have left the island since the eruptions began on 18 July 1995.

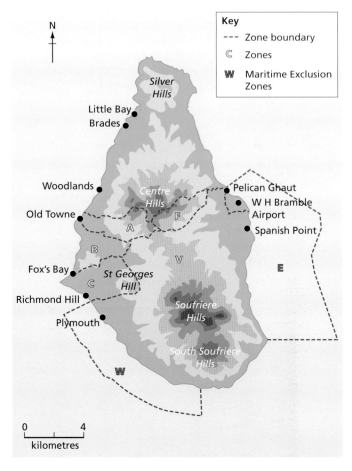

Figure 32 Hazard map for Montserrat

Activity

1 Study the article at the weblink on page 65.
  a) Describe three different types of activity which the scientists could have monitored.
  b) Suggest how the scientists could have used this data to keep people safe.

2 Look at the table below.
  a) Make a copy of the table.
  b) List the equipment used for each type of monitoring, some may have more than one method.
  c) Discuss what the advantages and disadvantages of each may be and fill in the columns.

3 Study Figure 32. The north part of the island is the safe zone.
  a) Roughly what percentage of the island is this?
  b) Why do you think there are maritime exclusion zones?
  c) The old capital Plymouth and W H Bramble airport had to be abandoned. What problems would this have caused for the people of Montserrat?

Type of monitoring	Equipment used	Advantages	Disadvantages
Seismic			
Deformation			
Gas readings			
Visual			

Hazard Level		1	2	3	4	5
Typical Activity		More than one year with no measured activity.	No activity that threatens the north or west. Low measured activity.	Mild activity that threatens the west. Significant change of measured activity. High measured activity.	Lava extrusion that threatens the north or west. Large unstable dome to the north or west.	Threat of large pyroclastic flows to the north or northwest. Threat of lateral blast or sector collapse.
Zones	A	Unrestricted	Unrestricted	Unrestricted	Unrestricted	Controlled access
	B	Unrestricted	Unrestricted	Unrestricted	Controlled access	Controlled access
	C	Unrestricted	Daytime access	Controlled access	Controlled access	Essential workers
	F	Unrestricted	Daytime access	Daytime access	Controlled access	Controlled access
	V	Daytime access to some areas	Controlled access	Essential workers	Essential workers	Essential workers
	T	Daytime access	Controlled access	Controlled access	Essential workers	Essential workers
Maritime Exclusion Zones	W	Unrestricted	Daytime access	Daytime access	Essential workers	Essential workers
	E	Unrestricted	Essential workers	Essential workers	Essential workers	Essential workers

Access Restrictions

Unrestricted – Ashfall and lahars can be significant hazards in all areas, and require appropriate precautions.

Daytime access – Access is permitted from 6:30am until 5:30pm. Access gates will be locked at all other times.

Daytime access to some areas – Areas will be defined depending on state and location of the volcanic activity.

Daytime transit – Boats permitted to travel through the MEZ without stopping from 6:30am until 5:30pm.

Controlled access – No access without approval from NDPRAC. Approval considered on a case-by-case basis. Gates will be locked at all times.

Essential workers – No access apart from MVO and associated staff. Access for essential maintenance only with approval from NDPRAC. Gates will be locked at all times.

Figure 33 Hazard alert table for Montserrat

www.mvo.ms/July_2008_Activity_this_week_archive.htm
Extract from a weekly activity report from the Montserrat Volcano Observatory

Soufriere Hills Volcano –
Weekly report update 18–25 July 2008

Activity at the Soufriere Hills Volcano increased during the past week, with mild eruptive activity, pyroclastic flows on the eastern flank of the volcano, and a noticeable increase in seismic activity.

This week, the MVO recorded 18 rockfalls and 145 earthquakes compared to 13 rockfalls and 8 earthquakes for the preceding week.

The average sulphur dioxide (SO_2) flux for the week was 378 tons per day (t/d). These are similar to last week's values.

The activity over the past few weeks shows continuing unrest at the volcano. Even if lava extrusion does not restart, the dome is still a very large mass of very hot material which is capable of collapsing or exploding at any time. Lahar activity in river valleys around the volcano is a potential hazard during and after periods of heavy rainfall.

Activity

4 a) Make a sketch map of Figure 32.
b) Using Figure 33 and the article at the above weblink colour code the map to show the hazard level on 18–25 July 2008.

5 What are the access restrictions for:
a) Plymouth
b) Old Towne?

6 Imagine you work for the Montserrat Volcano Observatory. Use the data from the article at the weblink to describe the action that should be taken in each of the areas shown on the hazard map of Montserrat.

Geography Futures

What would happen if the Yellowstone supervolcano erupted?

Underneath Yellowstone National Park in the USA sits a volcano so gigantic, that if it erupted it would have dramatic and far reaching consequences. This **supervolcano** is formed by magma rising up into the crust to form a vast underground reservoir 60 km long and 40 km wide. It is one of a handful of 'hot spot' volcanoes around the world. These occur on the interior of plates.

Every year, 3 million tourists visit the park, many to see the geothermal springs and geysers. Most are unaware that Yellowstone is an active volcano. Scientists are able to estimate that throughout history, Yellowstone has erupted every 600,000 years. It is 640,000 years since it last erupted. An eruption could be imminent!

The first signs of the eruption would be a huge earthquake felt across the USA. The blast would be heard around the world. Within a 1,000 km radius, the air would become choked with ash, suffocating people and animals. At least 90 per cent of the population would be killed. Rain would be black and acidic, killing most of the vegetation.

Within hours the east coast of the USA would have an ash cover of a few centimetres that would contaminate drinking water and destroy crops. Sunlight would be blocked by ash in the atmosphere. Travel could be hazardous as people start to panic and roads get busier.

After three or four days, Europe would have a fine ash cover. The sulphur gases in the atmosphere would lead to global cooling, plunging temperatures by up to 10 °C for about 10 years. Monsoon rains would fail, leading to famine across large parts of Asia. Overall, the global economy would be in turmoil. Food prices would soar leading to a strong possibility of conflicts over resources.

Figure 34 Yellowstone National Park with 1,000 km radius

Figure 35 A geyser, Yellowstone National Park

Activity

1 Using information on this page and your understanding, what would the human and environmental effects of an eruption be:
   a) within 1,000 km of Yellowstone?
   b) within the USA?
   c) globally?

2 Suggest how authorities could reduce the impact of a Yellowstone eruption.

3 Should we be worried about the consequences of an eruption at Yellowstone National Park? Write a 500-word report assessing the risks.

Where do people live?

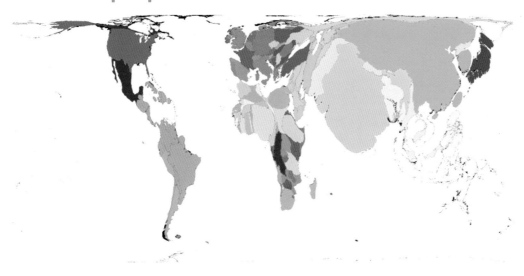

Figure 1 World population (2002 data). Each country is in proportion to the size of the population

GIS Activity: www.worldmapper.org

The Worldmapper website has a large collection of world maps that could be useful when studying Themes 4, 5 and 6. The maps have been drawn so that each country is in proportion to the data that is displayed. So, in Figure 1, countries such as Japan and China appear large because their populations are large.

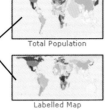

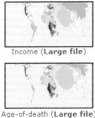

The easiest way to browse the site is to click on these thumbnails.

Use the search box if you know the number or name of a map.

Figure 2 The homepage of Worldmapper

Activity

1   Use the Worldmapper website to investigate:
   a) how population structure varies between MEDCs and LEDCs
   b) population change and future populations
   c) different causes of death in MEDCs and LEDCs.

To investigate	Category of maps	Use the following maps
Population structure	Basic	5, 6
Population change	Basic and cause of death	2, 8, 9, 10, 11, 12, 369, 370
Causes of death	Cause of death	374, 379, 389, 408, 418, 436, 451

Where do people live in the world?

The United Nations estimates that by 2008 more than half of the world's population will be living in urban areas: larger towns and cities. The urban population, which is the percentage of people living in towns and cities, has grown steadily since the 1950s:

- 30 per cent in 1950
- 47 per cent in 2000
- It is estimated that it will reach 60 per cent by 2030.

The process by which the population of a country becomes more urban and less rural is known as **urbanisation**. Urbanisation causes the physical and human growth of towns and cities. Urbanisation is caused by a combination of two factors:

- The migration of people from rural to urban areas.
- The natural increase of the urban population due to there being more births than deaths.

Figure 3 Most of the residents moving into UK cities are young professionals or students. So do we still need to provide the facilities needed by young families such as schools and safe open space?

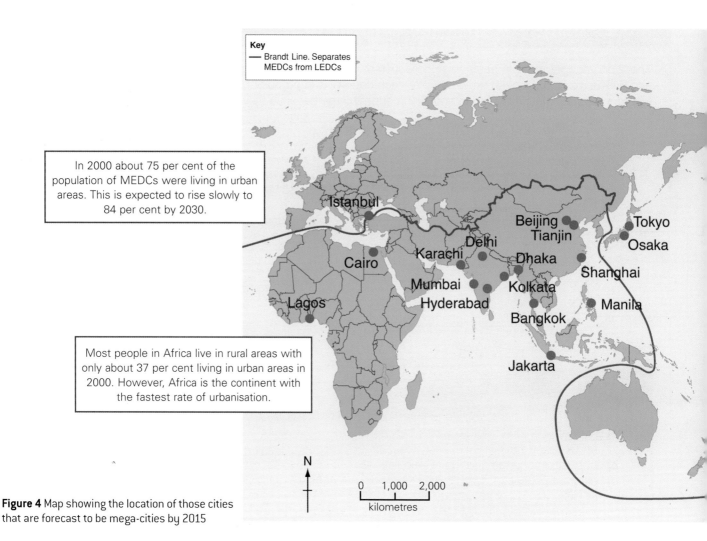

Key
— Brandt Line. Separates MEDCs from LEDCs

In 2000 about 75 per cent of the population of MEDCs were living in urban areas. This is expected to rise slowly to 84 per cent by 2030.

Most people in Africa live in rural areas with only about 37 per cent living in urban areas in 2000. However, Africa is the continent with the fastest rate of urbanisation.

N

0   1,000   2,000
kilometres

Figure 4 Map showing the location of those cities that are forecast to be mega-cities by 2015

Urbanisation is currently much more rapid in the Less Economically Developed Countries (LEDCs) than in More Economically Developed Countries (MEDCs). LEDCs tend to have faster-growing populations than MEDCs and they also have a larger number of people moving from rural to urban areas.

People move for a variety of reasons. Conflicts and natural disasters may force people to move, in which case the migrants may be described as **refugees**. However, in most cases people migrate out of choice rather than because of violence or disaster. People generally move because they want to improve their standard of living by finding a better-paid job. A migrant who moves in order to find work is described as an **economic migrant**. Many migrants also expect that moving to the city will improve their quality of life, perhaps by giving them better access to clean water or healthcare facilities.

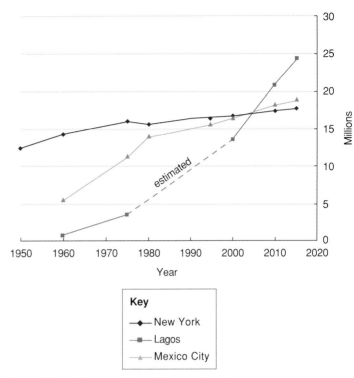

Figure 5 Growth in population of three major cities

Activity

1. Use Figure 4 to complete the following:
   MEDCs have a *larger / smaller* proportion of people living in urban areas than LEDCs. Of the less economically developed regions:
   - **............................. is the most urbanised**
   - **............................. is experiencing the most rapid urbanisation.**

2. Use the text on these pages to make your own definitions for **urbanisation, refugees** and **economic migrant**.

3. Explain the two factors that led to the more rapid urbanisation in LEDCs.

4. Use Figure 4.
   a) Describe the likely distribution of the world's mega-cities in 2015.
   b) Use Figure 5 to describe and explain the trend of each graph.

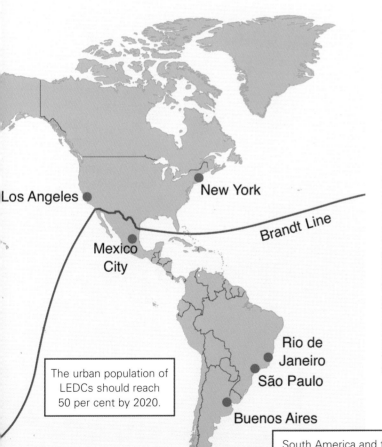

The urban population of LEDCs should reach 50 per cent by 2020.

South America and the Caribbean are the most urbanised part of the less economically developed world with about 75 per cent of the population living in urban areas.

Investigating rural to urban migration in South Africa

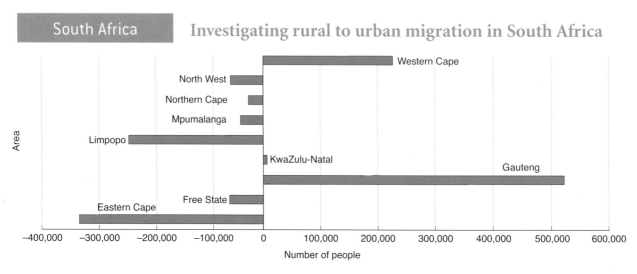

Figure 6 Total population gains and losses due to migration in 2005

Gauteng is South Africa's most urban province and contains three major cities of more than one million people: Johannesburg, Pretoria and Soweto. By contrast, the largest city in the neighbouring province of Limpopo has only 90,000 people and more than 90 per cent of the population lives in rural areas. In this case study we will investigate the reasons for migration between Limpopo and Gauteng, and also examine the effects of this migration on rural communities.

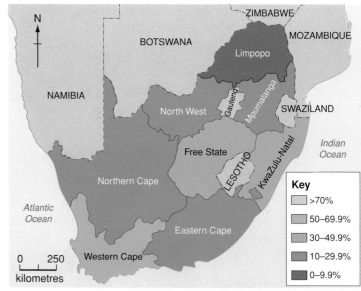

Figure 7 Urban population in South Africa's provinces (estimates based on population living in settlements greater than 20,000 people)

Activity

1 Use Figures 6 and 7 to complete the following:

The two most urban provinces are:

i) .... which gained .... migrants during 2005 and;

ii) .... which gained .... migrants in 2005. **The more rural provinces, such as ...., gained / lost population during the year.**

2 Study Figure 8. Choose from the following phrases to describe the flow of migrants from Limpopo:

Most migrants migrate short / long distances. Most / all migrants move to provinces that are less rural than Limpopo. Some / many migrants move to the most urban provinces of South Africa.

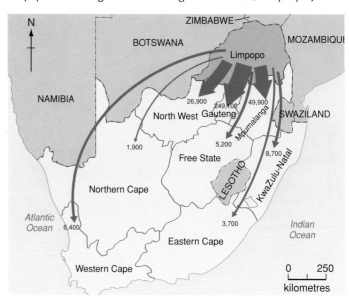

Figure 8 Migration from Limpopo province during 2005

What are the push/pull factors for rural to urban migration in South Africa?

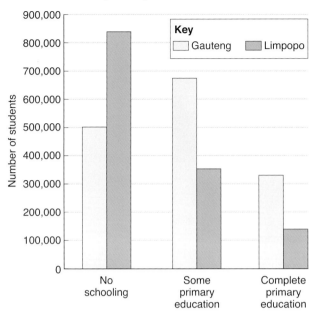

Figure 9 Comparing education in Limpopo with Gauteng

People living in rural areas such as Limpopo are attracted by the jobs and better opportunities available in cities such as Johannesburg. The possibility of better healthcare and schools for their children are pull factors that encourage migrants to leave their rural homes. At the same time, migrants are often dissatisfied with life in the countryside. Few rural houses have a connection to the national electricity grid. Most people do not own an electric cooker, let alone a computer or television. Lack of money, poor job opportunities and relatively low quality of life are all push factors that can force people to move away from rural areas.

People living in the province of Limpopo rely on either farming or tourism for their income. The region has a seasonal wet/dry tropical climate and a savanna ecosystem. Rural population densities are relatively high and farm sizes small.

Most households in Limpopo earn a little less than 1,000 Rand a month, whereas average household income in Johannesburg is 7,175 Rand a month. The poverty line in South Africa is defined at 1,100 Rand (about US$150) a month. Of people in Limpopo, 60 per cent live below this poverty line compared with only 20 per cent of people in Gauteng province.

Activity

3   Based on the evidence in Figures 6, 7 and 8:
    a) suggest why so few migrants move from Limpopo to Western Cape
    b) suggest which regions are losing migrants to Western Cape and give reasons for your answer.

4   Use Figure 9. How many students in each province:
    a) have no schooling
    b) complete primary education?

5   Explain how each of the following might be push factors that contribute to migration from rural areas of Limpopo.
    • The rural areas are densely populated.
    • Rainfall is low and unpredictable.
    • Rural communities are isolated from services such as schools and healthcare.

6   List the reasons for rural to urban migration using this table:

	Push factors	Pull factors
Economic reasons		
Education		
Quality of life		

The percentage of Johannesburg residents who:
• own an electric stove in the home: 77.86 per cent
• own a fridge or freezer: 87.26 per cent
• own a dishwasher: 5.24 per cent
• own a vacuum cleaner: 31.35 per cent
• own a television: 89.53 per cent
• own a hi-fi or music centre: 73.61 per cent
• own a personal computer: 17.86 per cent
• have a telephone connection: 57.65 per cent
• have eaten in a restaurant in the last month: 44.1 per cent
• bought a take-away meal in the last month (from a permanent establishment, not a street hawker): 55.26 per cent
• hired a video or DVD in the last month: 13.65 per cent.

Figure 10 Some lifestyle statistics for Johannesburg, drawn from the annual All Media Products Survey (AMPS)

7   Study Figure 10 taken from a South African website. Suggest how the internet and advertising might accidentally encourage further migration into Johannesburg.

South Africa   What are the consequences of rural to urban migration?

What effect does migration have on the rural areas that the migrants leave behind? Does the loss of so many people cause economic and social problems in the countryside? Or does migration create benefits for rural areas? Research suggests that the consequences of migration are very complex. They include:

• Brain drain – the loss of some of the most skilled workers.
• Remittances – the money sent back by workers to support their families.
• Information and ideas – new technologies and skills learned in the city flow back into the country where they are used to support local businesses.

www.statssa.gov.za/census2001/digiatlas/index.html
This site uses **Geographical Information Systems (GIS)** to display an online atlas of South Africa. It uses data from the most recent census which can be displayed in either map or graph form.

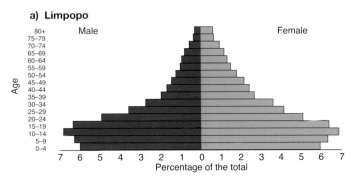

a) Limpopo

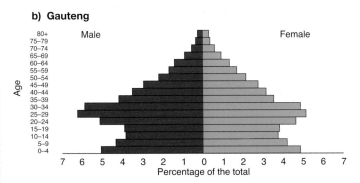

b) Gauteng

Figure 11 Population pyramids for a) Limpopo (a rural province) and b) Gauteng (a neighbouring urban province)

Activity

1 Compare the population pyramids in Figure 11. Focus on the differences/similarities in the following parts of each graph:
   a) The percentage of the population aged 0 to 19.
   b) The percentage of the population aged 25 to 34.
   c) The balance between males and females.

2 Use Figure 12 to suggest reasons for the differences you noticed between the population pyramids.

3 Explain whether each of the following is an advantage or disadvantage to a rural area that is losing migrants:
   a) brain drain
   b) remittances
   c) information and ideas.

Studies in South Africa show that:
• those aged between 15 and 35 are the most likely to migrate
• more males migrate than females, but an increasing number of females are migrating
• female migrants are slightly younger than male migrants
• circular migration (see page 73) is more common than permanent migration
• some rural migrants move to large urban areas such as Johannesburg, but many rural migrants move to smaller towns
• an increasing number of rural migrants move to other rural areas.

Figure 12 Key points of migration in South Africa

Circular migration

Many migrants do not make a permanent move to the city. It is common for people to leave the countryside when there are few farming jobs and return at busier times of the year, for example, at harvest. This temporary form of rural to urban migration is known as circular migration.

Circular migration brings both benefits and problems to rural communities. Migrants earn money which can be sent to the rural family and invested in improving the farm: repairing terraces and in tree-planting schemes. Circular migrants also reduce demand on village food and water supplies. This is particularly helpful in Limpopo which has a long dry season.

However, circular migration is almost certainly one of the reasons for the spread of AIDS and other sexually transmitted diseases. Studies in South Africa suggest that migrants are three times more likely to be infected with HIV than non-migrants. A returning migrant who is unaware that he or she is HIV positive could then infect a partner in the rural home. It is more difficult to treat rural AIDS sufferers because of their isolation from health clinics.

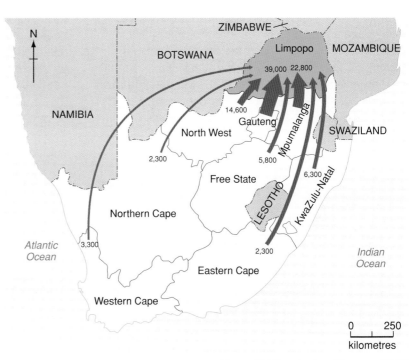

Figure 13 Migration into Limpopo, 2005

Activity

4 Define circular migration.

5 Use Figure 13.
   a) How many migrants returned from provinces that are mostly urban?
   b) Compare this map with Figure 8 on page 70. What are the similarities and differences?

6 Use the text and your own ideas to complete the following table about the advantages and disadvantages of circular migration.

	Advantages to the rural area	Disadvantages to the rural area
Economic		
Social		

7 Explain why circular migration is likely to be more beneficial to rural areas than permanent migration.

Why do people want to move from the city to the country in MEDCs?

The migration of people from larger cities into towns and villages in the countryside is a process known as **counter urbanisation**. This process has created enormous change in the rural areas of many MEDCs, especially in western Europe. Cities are often seen as stressful places in which to live and work. The cost and difficulty of commuting through rush hour traffic; the lack of open space and places for children to play safely; noise; pollution and rising crime are all given as reasons for leaving the city. By contrast, life in a smaller town or village has many attractions. People are drawn to the peace and quiet; access to open countryside can reduce stress and tension; and lower numbers of cars may seem safer for parents who have young children.

How has technology contributed to change in the countryside?

The move from town to country first became popular in the UK in the 1960s and 70s. This was a period of rising car ownership and expansion of the motorway network. It became possible to **commute** from a home in the country to a job in the city. Since then, massive changes in communication technology have made it possible for increasing numbers of people to work from a home in the country. Writers, researchers and business consultants can spend most of the working week at a computer at home and only need to commute to the office for the occasional meeting. This type of work is known as **tele-working** or tele-cottaging.

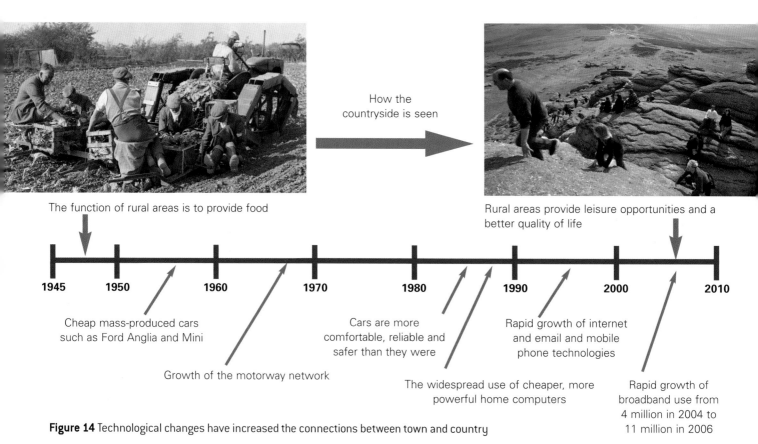

How the countryside is seen

The function of rural areas is to provide food

Rural areas provide leisure opportunities and a better quality of life

1945   1950   1960   1970   1980   1990   2000   2010

Cheap mass-produced cars such as Ford Anglia and Mini

Growth of the motorway network

Cars are more comfortable, reliable and safer than they were

The widespread use of cheaper, more powerful home computers

Rapid growth of internet and email and mobile phone technologies

Rapid growth of broadband use from 4 million in 2004 to 11 million in 2006

Figure 14 Technological changes have increased the connections between town and country

Activity

1 Study Figure 14. Use it to explain how technology has allowed:
  a) greater commuting
  b) greater use of the countryside for leisure
  c) more opportunities to move to the country and work from home.

2 Using Figure 14, suggest how you imagine the countryside might change 20 years from now.

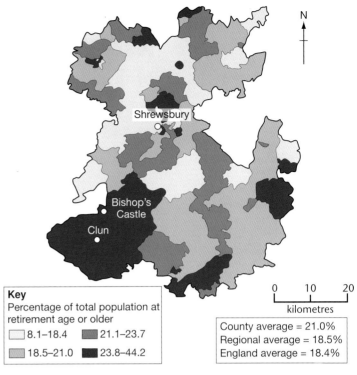

Shropshire · How are rural populations changing?

In South Shropshire, in the West Midlands, the relatively high **quality of life** in the countryside appeals to a wide range of people including young professionals, families and the retired. What these people have in common is the ability to pay the relatively high prices of rural homes. However, the countryside doesn't appeal to everyone. Many teenagers living in this area move to cities elsewhere in the UK when they leave school. The lack of jobs, leisure facilities, shops, theatres and cinemas in the countryside are push factors, while the chance to go to university and the greater choice of jobs are pull factors for moving to a city. In addition, the cost of buying a house in the countryside is likely to prevent young people on lower incomes from staying in a rural area. So, newcomers to rural life often have different social and economic (or **socio-economic**) backgrounds from the local people they replace.

Key
Percentage of total population at retirement age or older

8.1–18.4	21.1–23.7
18.5–21.0	23.8–44.2

County average = 21.0%
Regional average = 18.5%
England average = 18.4%

Figure 15 Patterns of retirement in Shropshire in different wards

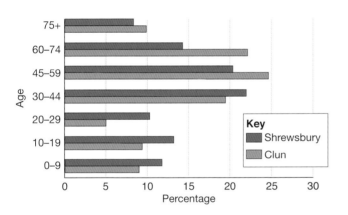

Figure 16 Comparing population structures in Shrewsbury and Clun

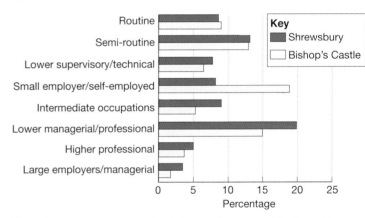

Figure 17 Comparing occupations in Shrewsbury and Bishop's Castle (Source: 2001 Census)

Activity

3 Use Figure 15 to describe the distribution of wards that have more than 23.8 per cent retired population.

4 Use Figure 16.
   a) Compare the population structure of Clun to that of Shrewsbury.
   b) Suggest two reasons for the differences you have noticed.

5 Use Figure 17.
   a) Compare occupations in Bishop's Castle and Shrewsbury.
   b) Use this evidence to explain why some younger adults are leaving south Shropshire.

6 Draw up a table like the one below. Add to the push and pull factors that cause movements in and out of rural areas like Shropshire.

Retired professional moving out of larger towns and into the countryside		Young adult moving out of the countryside and into larger towns	
Push factors	Pull factors	Push factors	Pull factors
	Peace and quiet	Few full-time jobs	

What will happen to the world population?

What factors influence birth and death rates?

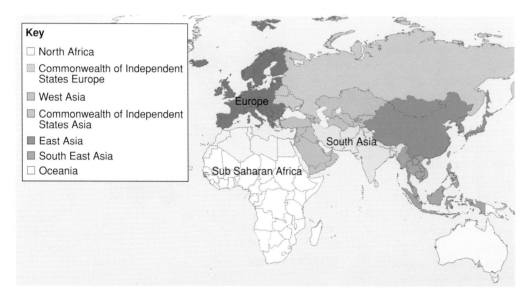

Key
- ☐ North Africa
- ▨ Commonwealth of Independent States Europe
- ▨ West Asia
- ▨ Commonwealth of Independent States Asia
- ▨ East Asia
- ▨ South East Asia
- ☐ Oceania

Europe

South Asia

Sub Saharan Africa

Figure 18 This map shows how the UN groups countries into regions

In this chapter we will investigate how population is changing in three very different regions of the world: sub-Saharan Africa, Europe and South Asia.

Birth rates are affected by a wide range of factors which include:

- family income – poor families are generally larger
- access to family planning services
- levels of female education – better educated women tend to have smaller families
- government policies on health, education and family planning.

Poverty has a dramatic influence on the birth rate. The poorest parents regard their children as an asset. Their children can help support the family by doing chores around the home and looking after younger brother or sisters. Children can be sent out to work and help support family income. When poor parents are elderly they can rely on their children to support them, even if they have no savings or a pension.

Where family planning services are readily available, birth rates are lower than areas where access is limited. To combat the higher birth rates in remote, rural areas, outreach health schemes operate. In some communities family planning is hampered by social or religious factors. For example, in some societies it is the father who decides how large the family should be and women have little or no say in this decision. In addition, some religions discourage the use of contraception. A good education, particularly amongst women, leads to a lower birth rate as women have better employment

opportunities and are more educated about family planning services. Fertility can be influenced by government policies. In China the current birth rate is estimated at 13.5 per 1,000 population compared with 33.6 per 1,000 in 1970. The birth rate fell dramatically because of the 'One Child Policy'. This is a hardline government policy introduced by the Chinese authorities in 1979 to reduce population growth. Other countries have adopted policies in an attempt to increase their birth rate.

Good nutrition, clean drinking water and good **primary health care** are all factors that help reduce the death rate. Primary health care includes preventing illness through immunisation and education as well as treatment of people who are ill. Having good access to primary health care means that people are able to get the treatment they need when they need it, even if they live in remote rural areas. HIV and malaria are two diseases that have an unusually high impact on death rates in some countries. Malaria kills over one million people a year with 90 per cent of deaths occurring in Africa. The highest death rates in rural Africa occur where there are problems in distributing the preventative drugs.

High death rates do not automatically mean that a country has poor health care systems. The death rate of a country will automatically be higher where the population has a high proportion of elderly people. When the death rate is higher than the birth rate the population will begin to decrease. This is beginning to happen in some MEDCs such as Russia.

Selected countries		Birth rate	Death rate	Fertility	Infant mortality	GNI (US$)
Sub-Saharan Africa	Malawi	46	18	6.3	96	250
	Mali	48	16	6.6	96	500
	Ghana	33	10	4.4	59	590
	Kenya	40	12	4.9	77	680
	South Africa	23	15	2.7	43	5,750
Europe	Russia	10	15	1.3	10	7,560
	Italy	10	9	1.4	3.7	33,540
	Germany	8	10	1.3	3.8	38,860
	UK	12	10	1.6	4	42,740
	Iceland	15	6	2.1	2.4	54,100
South Asia	Bangladesh	27	8	3.0	65	470
	Pakistan	31	8	4.1	78	870
	India	24	8	2.9	58	950
	Sri Lanka	18	7	2.0	11	1,540
	Bhutan	20	7	2.9	40	1,770

Figure 19 Population data for selected regions featured in this chapter (all figures 2007)

Birth rate	The number of births in one year for every 1,000 population
Death rate	The number of deaths in one year for every 1,000 population
Fertility	The average number of children in a family
Infant mortality	The number of deaths of children before the age of one for every 1,000 births
GNI	Gross National Income. A measure of average income per person, measured in US dollars.

Figure 20 Definitions for population and development data

Activity

1 Use an atlas and Figure 18 to name three other countries in sub-Saharan Africa and three in South Asia that are not listed in Figure 19.

2 Use Figure 19.
  a) Plot pairs of bar graphs for each country showing birth and death rates.
  b) Which countries have the biggest gap between birth and death rates?
  c) In which countries are death rates higher than birth rates?
  d) Suggest why some governments are keen to increase birth rates.

3 Use evidence from Figure 19 to explain which region has the best and worst health care systems.

4 Use Figure 19 to examine the relationship between fertility and GNI. You could plot a scattergraph. Alternatively, draw bar graphs to compare the two sets of data. What conclusion do you come to?

5 Work in pairs.
  a) For a country like Malawi, outline five things the government could do to reduce birth and death rates.
  b) Explain each of your strategies to another pair of students.
  c) Working as a four, agree on your three most important strategies.

Examiner's Tips

Understanding command words

It is important to read and understand the question asked. You will be keen to get on with the exam paper but it is a wise investment of time to consider the demands of the question and ensure you answer all parts of the question. Command words are the words in a question that tell you what the examiner is looking for. The examiner will mark only the parts of your answer that are relevant to the question.

Compare and Annotate

Compare is a command word that demands that you think in a comparative way. You may be required to compare two graphs, two sets of figures, two countries, two photographs or two maps. It is important that you describe how the resources are both similar and different from one another. The common mistake is to describe the two resources separately.

Annotate means that you must add explanatory notes to a diagram, graph, map or photograph. An annotation has explanation, whereas a label is a simple description.

Sample question 1

Annotate the population pyramid for the UK to explain the main features of its population structure. [4]

Student Answer

What the examiner has to say!

This may seem harsh but I would give this candidate only 2 marks. Labelling is excellent but there are only two explanatory statements here.

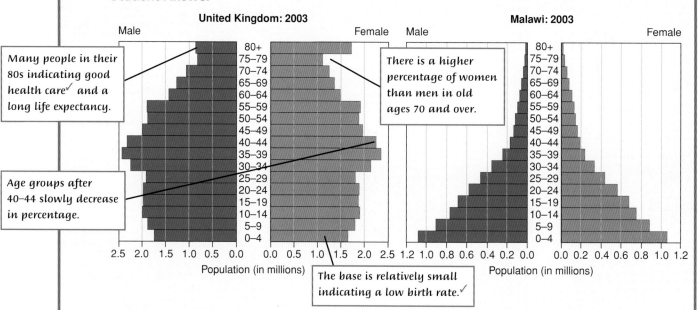

United Kingdom: 2003

Many people in their 80s indicating good health care✓ and a long life expectancy.

Age groups after 40–44 slowly decrease in percentage.

There is a higher percentage of women than men in old ages 70 and over.

The base is relatively small indicating a low birth rate.✓

Malawi: 2003

Sample question 2

Compare and contrast the population structure of the UK with that of Malawi. [6]

Student answer

In Malawi there is a much younger population✓ as the birth rate is high and the death rate is high. There is a high amount of people in their 30s in the UK whereas there are fewer middle-aged people in Malawi.✓ In both population pyramids there are fewer old people.✓ In Malawi the structure of the pyramid is steadily decreasing as you go up the age groups while in the UK the structure is fairly random below the age of 50 and only starts to steadily decrease

after 50.✓ Both the male and female population are about the same for each country✓ although the UK has many more people living past 80.✓ Malawi is more pyramid shaped✓ and typical of an LEDC.

What the examiner has to say!

This is a good quality answer worth 6 marks. The candidate clearly understands the demands of the question. The candidate uses many comparative statements such as: younger, whereas, both, while and although. The question does not ask for an explanation so the reference to high birth rates and death rates typical of an LEDC is good geography but does not score a mark.

Exam practice

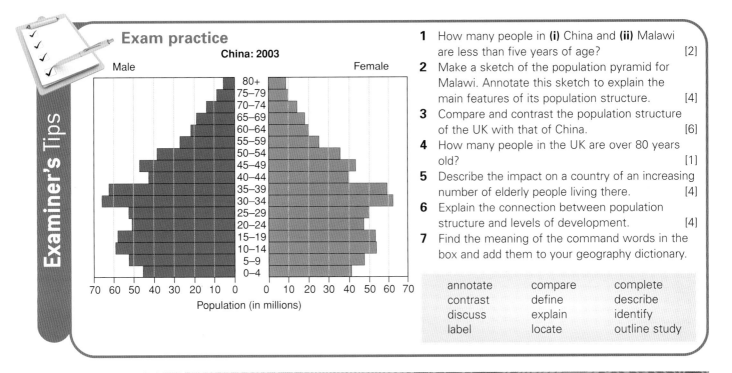

China: 2003

Male   Female

Population (in millions)

1   How many people in (i) China and (ii) Malawi are less than five years of age?   [2]
2   Make a sketch of the population pyramid for Malawi. Annotate this sketch to explain the main features of its population structure.   [4]
3   Compare and contrast the population structure of the UK with that of China.   [6]
4   How many people in the UK are over 80 years old?   [1]
5   Describe the impact on a country of an increasing number of elderly people living there.   [4]
6   Explain the connection between population structure and levels of development.   [4]
7   Find the meaning of the command words in the box and add them to your geography dictionary.

annotate	compare	complete
contrast	define	describe
discuss	explain	identify
label	locate	outline study

Examiner's Tips

GIS Activity: National Statistics website

www.statistics.gov.uk/census2001/pyramids/pages/uk.asp

The National Statistics website is an official UK government site for the UK census. The data includes all sorts of population data and shows population pyramids for many regions of the UK. The link above will take you to the screen shown in Figure 21. Click on one of the links to a national level or an English region to view pyramids for other parts of the UK.

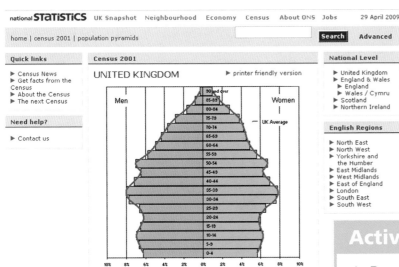

Figure 21 A screenshot showing the UK population pyramid. Clicking on the link to South West in the list of English regions will open a screen with further links shown in Figure 24. Each of these links will allow you to view a new pyramid

Figure 22 Some of the options that open when you follow the link to South West

Activity

1   Research population pyramids for different areas of the UK, e.g. Cardiff, Cornwall, Gwynedd, Pembrokeshire, south Shropshire and London. Compare and contrast these pyramids and explain their different structures.

Population issues in South Asia

Poverty and fertility in South Asia are still relatively high. The region already has 24 per cent of the world's population and this percentage is predicted to rise to 27 per cent by 2050. Patterns of fertility vary considerably within South Asian countries. The poorest families are larger because poor parents regard their children as an asset who can help support the family income. Grown-up children are also expected to support elderly parents who, in poorer families, have few savings and no pension. So, the region faces a number of issues. How to:

- encourage family planning to slow population growth
- improve standards of health care for mothers and children
- raise the status of women and improve education for girls.

	Population (2007)	Projected population (2025)	Projected population (2050)
Iran	71.2	88.2	100.2
Afghanistan	31.9	50.3	81.9
Pakistan	169.3	228.8	295.0
India	1131.9	1391.2	1747.3
Sri Lanka	20.1	21.2	19.5
Bangladesh	149.0	190.0	231.0
Bhutan	0.9	1.1	1.3
Nepal	27.8	36.1	42.6
Total South Asia	**1602.1**	**2006.9**	**2518.8**

Figure 23 Population and predicted population for South Asian countries

Activity

1 Use Figure 23.
   a) Choose an appropriate style of graph to plot the population growth of each country.
   b) Describe the trend on your graphs. Which countries will experience most growth?
   c) Using this evidence, suggest which country has the most effective family planning policies.

2 a) Study Figure 24 and describe the distribution of states which have a fertility:
      i) higher than 3
      ii) lower than 2,
   b) Explain how improving access to regular pay and improved education could reduce fertility.

3 Use the data in Figure 25 to investigate each of the following enquiries:
   a) Do states with higher levels of female literacy have lower fertility?
   b) Is fertility higher in those states with more poor households (indicated by lower percentages of houses with electricity)?
   c) Do the states with low status for women (indicated by low sex ratios) also have higher fertility?

India — Investigating patterns of fertility in India

Fertility within India varies considerably from state to state. This pattern may be explained by:

- variations in family income with some states having more opportunities for regularly paid jobs than others
- better education for girls in some states means that young women delay having their first child in order to take paid work and pursue a career (see page 123).

In some parts of South Asia, including some Indian states, daughters have lower status than sons. In a poor household this may mean that girls have fewer educational opportunities than boys. Girls from poor households with little education often marry young. These young women then have large families because that is what their husbands want. Furthermore, poor families may prefer to have sons rather than daughters because a son will help support family income. In some cases this leads to women terminating their pregnancies if they discover they are carrying a daughter. In other cases, young girls suffer neglect and die. This explains why there are fewer women than men in most Indian states.

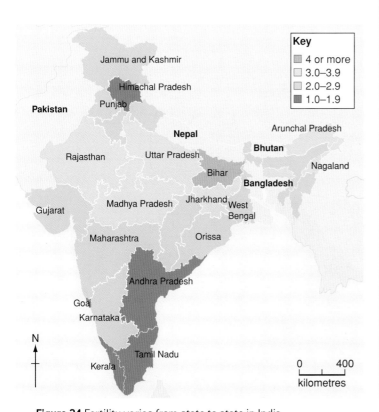

Figure 24 Fertility varies from state to state in India

State	Sex ratio	Female literacy	Fertility	Percentage homes with electricity
Andhra Pradesh	978	50.4	1.8	88.4
Arunachal Pradesh	893	43.5	3.0	76.9
Assam	935	54.6	2.4	38.1
Bihar	919	33.1	4.0	27.7
Chhattisgarh	989	51.9	2.6	71.4
Goa	961	75.4	1.8	96.4
Gujarat	920	57.8	2.4	89.3
Haryana	861	55.7	2.7	91.5
Himachal Pradesh	968	67.4	1.9	98.5
Jammu & Kashmir	892	43.0	2.4	93.2
Jharkhand	941	38.9	3.3	40.2
Karnataka	965	56.9	2.1	89.3
Kerala	1,058	87.7	1.9	91.0
Madhya Pradesh	919	50.3	3.1	71.4
Maharastra	922	67.0	2.1	83.5
Manipur	974	56.8	2.8	87.0
Meghalaya	972	59.6	3.8	70.4
Mizoram	935	86.7	2.9	92.3
Nagaland	900	61.5	3.7	82.9
Orissa	972	50.5	2.4	45.4
Punjab	876	63.4	2.0	96.3
Rajasthan	921	43.9	3.2	66.1
Sikkim	875	60.4	2.0	92.1
Tamil Nadu	987	64.4	1.8	88.6
Tripura	948	64.9	2.4	68.8
Uttar Pradesh	898	42.2	3.8	42.8
Uttaranchal	962	59.6	2.6	80.0
West Bengal	934	59.6	2.3	52.5

Figure 25 Selected data for Indian states. The sex ratio is the number of women for every 1,000 men. Female literacy is the percentage of women who can read and write

Population issues in sub-Saharan Africa

Sub-Saharan Africa is the world's poorest region. Within this region there are some countries that have made good progress at reducing poverty. Countries such as Mauritius and, to a lesser extent, South Africa, have seen improvements in incomes, health care and education. However, the region has the highest infant mortality rates in the world and, as Figure 26 shows, they are only coming down slowly. A key population issue for Africa is to reduce infant mortality and improve primary health care. How can this be done?

Investigating the impact of malaria

Malaria is spread by mosquitoes carrying a parasite that infects a person when bitten. It is an entirely preventable disease. However, every year 300 million people get malaria resulting in over 1 million deaths worldwide. Malaria is a health threat in tropical regions of the world. Around 40 per cent of the world's population live in areas where malaria is **endemic** (i.e. malaria is constantly present) but 90 per cent of deaths occur in sub-Saharan Africa.

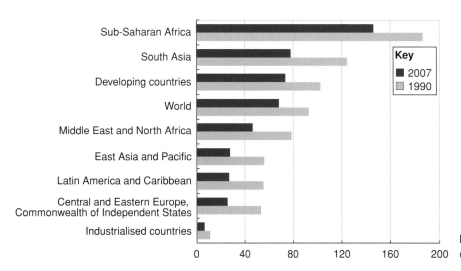

Figure 26 Infant mortality rates (deaths of children under 1 for every 1,000 births)

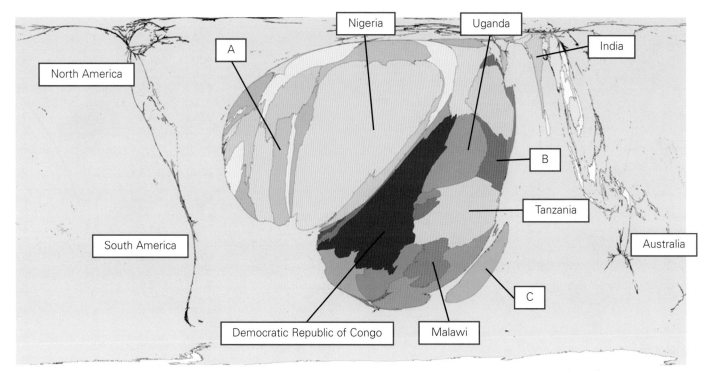

Figure 27 Deaths from malaria. Countries are shown in proportion to the number of deaths from malaria in one year (2002)

Malawi

Case study of malaria in Malawi

Malaria is one of Malawi's most serious heath problems. In Malawi, the risk from malaria varies across the country and also throughout the year. The shores of Lake Malawi provide ideal breeding conditions for mosquitoes, with warm temperatures and stagnant water. The highland areas are generally cooler and drier. Here, malaria is seasonal with cases reaching a peak during the rainy season when ditches and puddles quickly form and attract mosquitoes. Around 83 per cent of Malawi's population live in rural areas. Deaths from malaria are significantly higher in rural areas than they are in the cities of Blantyre and Lilongwe. Houses in rural areas are constructed of mud bricks with thatched roofs and offer little protection from mosquitoes.

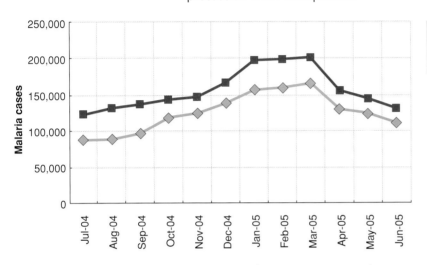

Figure 28 New malaria cases per month in Malawi (July 2004–June 2005)

	Mean minimum temp (Celsius)	Mean maximum temp (Celsius)	Average precipitation (mm)
Jan	17	27	208
Feb	17	27	218
March	16	27	125
April	14	27	43
May	11	25	3
June	8	23	0
July	7	23	0
Aug	8	25	0
Sept	12	27	0
Oct	15	30	0
Nov	17	29	53
Dec	18	28	125

Figure 29 Climate for Lilongwe, Malawi

Activity

1 Use Figure 27 and an atlas to find out:
   a) which tropical region has very few cases of malaria?
   b) the names of countries A, B and C
   c) which region of the world, after sub-Saharan Africa, has the next largest number of cases of malaria?

2 Describe the annual pattern of new malaria cases for children under five. Refer to figures in your answer.

3 Use Figure 29.
   a) Draw a climate chart for Malawi.
   b) Describe the annual pattern of rainfall.

4 Using evidence from Figures 28 and 29, explain why new cases of malaria are more common at certain times of the year.

Malawi — Are some people at more risk from malaria than others?

The health risks of malaria vary widely for different groups of people. Not everyone who catches malaria will die. In fact, over time, continued infection from mosquito bites will lead to a person becoming immune. Prevalence rates in Malawi show that 60 per cent of babies and children under three years old had malaria compared with only 12 per cent for adult men. As children and adults age, they develop resistance to the disease and the numbers of deaths go down.

Some people are at greater risk of death from malaria than others. The groups at highest risk are children and pregnant women, especially those in their first pregnancy. Around 40 per cent of child deaths (children under five) are from malaria. People with poor immune systems are at high risk. It is estimated that 12 per cent of Malawi's population is living with the HIV virus, which destroys a person's immune system. They are unable to fend off diseases and the death rate from malaria is higher than for people without HIV. Pregnancy also leads to a slight decline in immunity levels. This results in slightly more pregnant women dying from the disease than non-pregnant women.

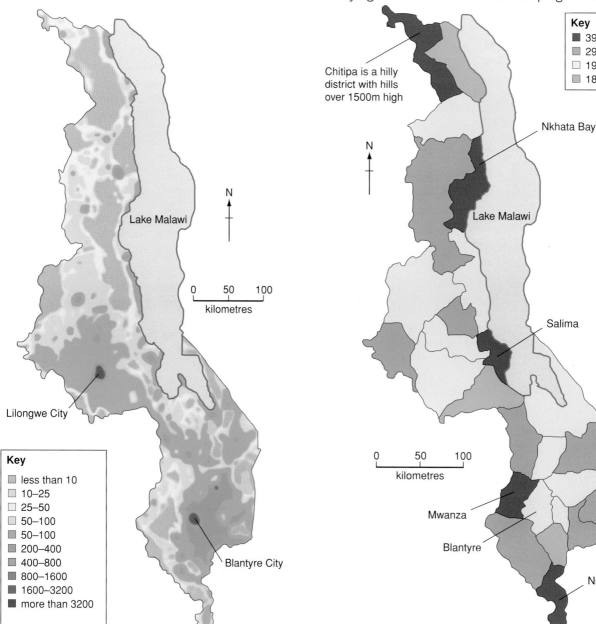

Chitipa is a hilly district with hills over 1500m high

Nkhata Bay

Lake Malawi

Salima

Mwanza

Blantyre

Nsanje

Key
- 39% or more
- 29–38%
- 19–28%
- 18% or less

Lake Malawi

Lilongwe City

Blantyre City

Key
- less than 10
- 10–25
- 25–50
- 50–100
- 50–100
- 200–400
- 400–800
- 800–1600
- 1600–3200
- more than 3200

Figure 30 Population densities in Malawi. Rural areas generally have lower population densities than urban areas

Figure 31 Distribution of malaria in Malawi (on average 28% of the population have malaria)

Strategies to combat malaria

A number of strategies have been implemented in Malawi to combat the disease. In 2000, the Millennium Development Goals (MDGs) were adopted by governments around the world. One of the goals was to reduce the number of cases of malaria by 2015. One way this goal can be reached is by encouraging the use of Insecticide Treated Bed nets (ITNs). This is a very effective way of reducing incidents of malaria and is relatively cheap. Each bed net costs only £3. However, many people in rural Malawi are unable to afford this. In the last 15 years, the Ministry of Health, and charities such as Nothing but Nets, have distributed bed nets across Malawi. In 1997 only 8 per cent of homes in Malawi had bed nets. By 2004 the average was 50 per cent. To maintain effectiveness, nets need to be retreated every 6–12 months and this is something that is easily forgotten.

Insecticides are sprayed in areas where mosquitoes are likely to come into contact with humans. The problem is that mosquitoes have developed a resistance to insecticides and they aren't as effective as they could be. Similarly the malaria parasite has become resistant to drugs. New drugs need to be developed urgently. Once a person starts to show signs of malaria, they need to take anti-malarial drugs as soon as possible to stand a better chance of fighting the disease. Unfortunately, not everyone in Malawi is able to access drugs when they need them. This is often because people living in rural areas have to travel a long way to reach a doctor. Also, because the early symptoms of malaria are similar to many other conditions, people often don't realise until it's too late. Malaria has the biggest impact on poor people, as they cannot afford to buy nets and get the treatment they need. It can become a vicious circle where people are prevented from getting out of poverty because of the burden malaria has on their lives.

Figure 32 Deaths due to malaria can be prevented using Insecticide Treated Bed nets (ITNs)

Activity

1 **a)** Identify which three groups of people are most at risk from malaria.
  b) Explain why some people are more at risk than others.

2 **a)** Use Figure 31 to describe the distribution of malaria in Malawi.
  b) Use evidence from the text on pages 83–84 to suggest different reasons for the high rates of malaria in two of the named districts on Figure 31.
  c) Compare Figures 30 and 31. Use these maps to provide evidence that malaria is more common in rural areas.

3 Produce a short newspaper article. Use the following as a headline: 'Malaria, the forgotten killer'.

4 Work in pairs. Discuss each of the following and then summarise your conclusions in two spider diagrams.
  a) Does malaria cause poverty or is it a result of poverty?
  b) Which groups should be targeted for ITNs?

GIS Activity: Population Action website

www.populationaction.org/Publications/Reports/The_Shape_of_Things_to_Come_Interactive_Database/Index.shtml

Population Action International is a non-profit **Non-Government Organisation (NGO)** that supports family planning programmes. It has a useful interactive database on its website that allows you to:

- view maps of population structure now and in 2050
- compare population pyramids for up to three different countries at a time
- investigate how population structures will change.

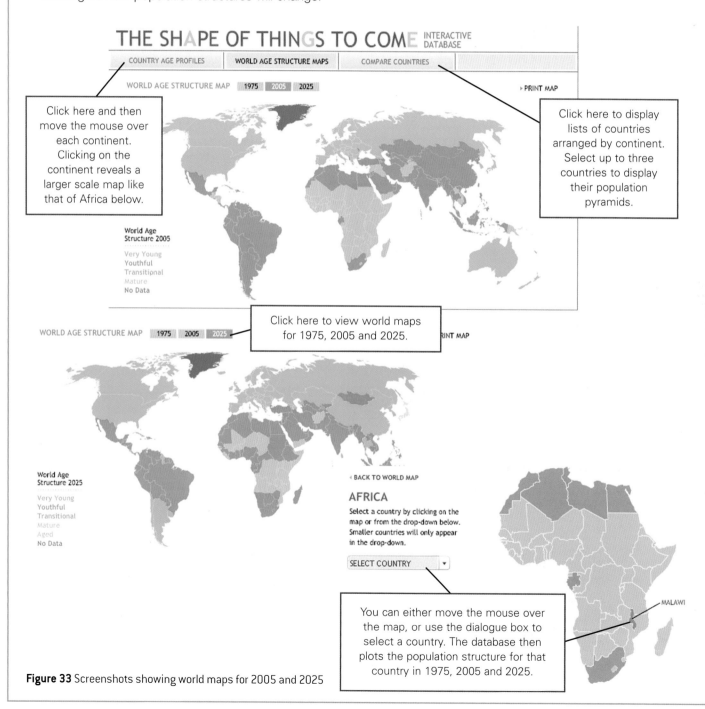

Figure 33 Screenshots showing world maps for 2005 and 2025

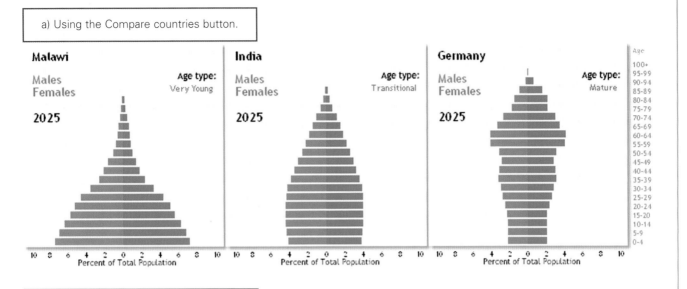

a) Using the Compare countries button.

b) Using the Country Age Profiles button.

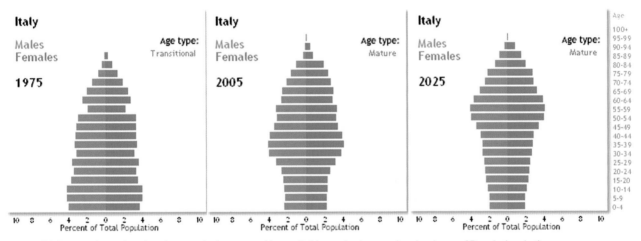

Figure 34 Screenshots showing the population pyramids available on the interactive database of Population Action

Activity

1 a) Which region in the world has most countries with a very young population on both maps?

   b) Which country has an aged population?

   c) Compare the two maps in Figure 33. Focus on the similarities and differences in countries with:
- **i)** very young populations
- **ii)** transitional populations.

2 Use Figure 34 a).

   a) Describe and explain the differences between the three countries in Figure 34 a).

   b) Describe and explain how Italy's population structure is changing in Figure 34 b).

   c) Suggest how Italy's population structure may cause problems for this country in the future.

3 a) Use the Population Action website to investigate how the population structure of each of the following countries will change in the future.
- **i)** Russia   **ii)** Malawi   **iii)** India.

   b) For each of these countries explain what you consider to be their biggest population challenge in the future.

Geography Futures

How will populations change in the future?

We have seen that fertility is falling in most countries and that improvement to primary health care means that people are living longer than before. This means that the next challenge to face many governments is the ageing of their population. Living longer creates many challenges for society. This is particularly true in European countries where the number of elderly people is growing rapidly.

- Who should care for the retired and elderly in society? Should families take the responsibility or should the government care for us when we are too old to care for ourselves? Will our savings and pension be enough to fund our increasingly long life between retirement and death?
- Will there be enough younger adults to do the work needed to keep the economy running? In a rich and successful economy like that of the UK, Italy or Germany, who will do the dirty, difficult and dangerous jobs that are badly paid and which no one really wants?
- What will be the impact on the health service as more people require increasingly expensive treatments?

	Selected countries	Number aged 60 or over (1,000s)		Percentage aged 60 or over	
		2006	2050	2006	2050
Sub-Saharan Africa	Malawi	615	1,734	5	6
	Mali	581	2,630	4	6
	Ghana	1,302	5,555	6	14
	Kenya	1,440	8,223	4	10
	South Africa	3,327	6,352	7	13
Europe	Russia	24,282	34,755	17	31
	Italy	15,109	21,051	26	41
	Germany	20,864	27,572	25	35
	UK	12,837	19,741	21	29
	Iceland	641	1,859	15	32
South Asia	Bangladesh	8,264	40,672	6	17
	Pakistan	9,445	46,745	6	15
	India	89,992	329,683	8	21
	Sri Lanka	2,284	6,919	11	29
	Bhutan	156	646	7	15

Figure 35 The ageing population

Activity

1 Study Figure 35.
   a) Which region will have the lowest percentage of its population aged over 60 in 2050?
   b) Which country:
      i) will have the largest percentage of people aged over 60 in 2050?
      ii) will have the biggest percentage increase of those aged over 60 between 2006 and 2050?

What is globalisation?

How have changes in business and technology increased interdependence?

This theme is about the global economy. Flows of people, ideas, money and goods are making an increasingly complex global web of interdependence that links together people and places from distant continents. We call this process **globalisation**.

Figure 1 The factors that drive globalisation

Example: avocados grown in Mexico will be flown to a UK supermarket. This improves customer choice but food air miles have an impact on carbon emissions.

Example: local people demonstrating about the falling water levels in their wells after this soft-drinks company opened a bottling plant in Kerala, India.

Multi-national companies: Large companies open branches in several different countries throughout the world.

The factors that drive globalisation

Trade: Improved technology and cheap aviation fuel mean that fresh food can be flown from distant places to our supermarkets.

Ideas and communication: The growth of communication technology such as the internet, mobile phones and satellite television has vastly improved global interdependence.

Culture: Certain styles of music, television and film are now shown around the world.

Example: films made in Hollywood, USA, advertised in an Asian street. But will local styles of music and entertainment survive?

Example: African countries that have few telephone landlines have used mobile technology to leapfrog the problem.

Investigating the role of multi-national companies in the global world of business

The world is increasingly interdependent: more and more places are being linked together by flows of money, ideas and goods. Key players in the process of globalisation have been multi-national companies (MNCs), or trans-national companies (TNCs).

Products such as soft drinks, fast food, mobile phones and clothing have global appeal and a global marketplace. The production and sale of these consumer goods is dominated by a relatively small number of manufacturers known as multi-national companies. For a company to be defined as an MNC it has to have branches in more than one country. The branches of an MNC include offices, factories and research and development (R&D) laboratories. Why do MNCs have branches located in different countries?

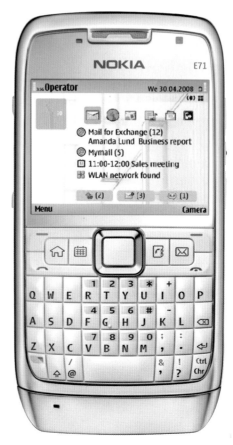

Figure 2 A mobile phone: a multi-national product

a) Sales by region in 2007

Key
Europe
Asia Pacific
Middle East and Africa
China
Latin America
North America

4%
8%
13%
39%
14%
22%

b) Employees by region in 2007

Key
Europe
Asia Pacific
China
Latin America
North America
Middle East and Africa

5% 4%
11%
12%
52%
16%

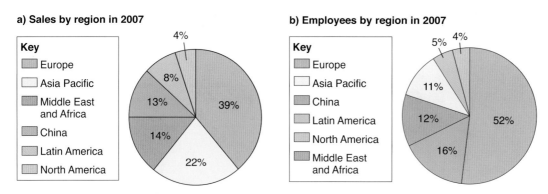

Figure 3 Nokia's sales (a) and employees (b) by region, December 2007

Activity

1 Study Figures 3 and 4 and complete the following description:

Fifty-two per cent of Nokia's employees work in the continent of …. A total of … per cent of their employees work in China and the Asia Pacific region. Many of these work in … industries making items such as … and …. Most of Nokia's sales are in …. Second is the Asia Pacific region with … per cent of sales.

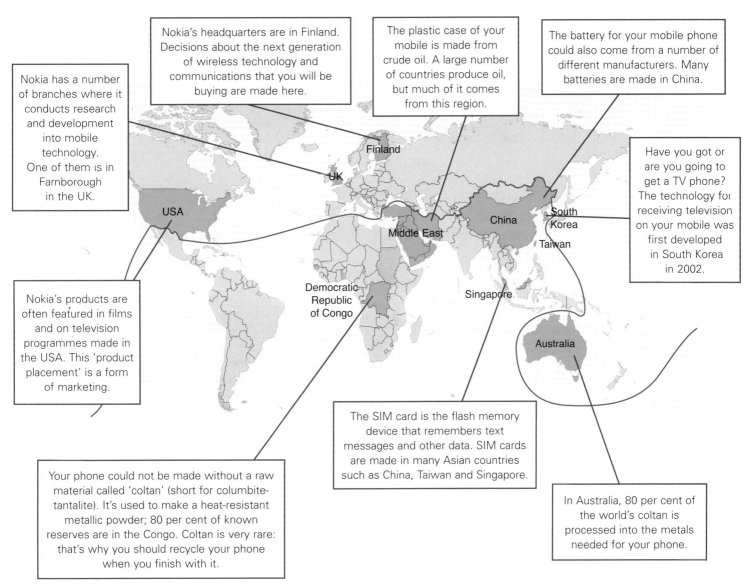

Nokia's headquarters are in Finland. Decisions about the next generation of wireless technology and communications that you will be buying are made here.

The plastic case of your mobile is made from crude oil. A large number of countries produce oil, but much of it comes from this region.

The battery for your mobile phone could also come from a number of different manufacturers. Many batteries are made in China.

Nokia has a number of branches where it conducts research and development into mobile technology. One of them is in Farnborough in the UK.

Have you got or are you going to get a TV phone? The technology for receiving television on your mobile was first developed in South Korea in 2002.

Nokia's products are often featured in films and on television programmes made in the USA. This 'product placement' is a form of marketing.

Finland

UK

USA

China

South Korea

Middle East

Taiwan

Democratic Republic of Congo

Singapore

Australia

The SIM card is the flash memory device that remembers text messages and other data. SIM cards are made in many Asian countries such as China, Taiwan and Singapore.

Your phone could not be made without a raw material called 'coltan' (short for columbite-tantalite). It's used to make a heat-resistant metallic powder; 80 per cent of known reserves are in the Congo. Coltan is very rare: that's why you should recycle your phone when you finish with it.

In Australia, 80 per cent of the world's coltan is processed into the metals needed for your phone.

Figure 4 The world in your mobile phone

Activity

2 Study Figure 4 and use it to complete a table like the one below:

Type of employment	Example	Place	MEDC or LEDC
Primary	1 Drilling for oil 2		
Secondary	1 Processing coltan 2	China	LEDC
Tertiary	1 2		

3 Work in pairs to structure a globalisation enquiry.
   a) Choose one of these titles: 'World in your living room' or 'World in your wardrobe'.
   b) Discuss all the different places you might find 'Made in…' information.
   c) Design a data collection sheet that you could use to record results from your classmates.
   d) Collect the data from at least five classmates and plot the data on a world outline map or make a large poster with photos you have collected from magazines or the internet.

4 Suggest why Nokia equips its phones with SIM cards and batteries made by a number of different manufacturers in Asia.

Nokia

A case study of a multi-national company

Nokia is the world's largest manufacturer of mobile phones and other mobile devices. It also provides network and communication services to other businesses, improving communications. Nokia is a Finnish MNC. Its head office is in Helsinki, Finland, but it has offices and factories all around the globe. Nokia and Nokia Siemens Networks employ more than 112,000 people worldwide. Nokia has plants (offices, factories and laboratories) in many different countries:

- research and development laboratories (R&D) in ten countries employing 30,415 people
- factories in ten countries
- sales offices in more than 150 countries.

Why does Nokia have plants located in so many different countries?

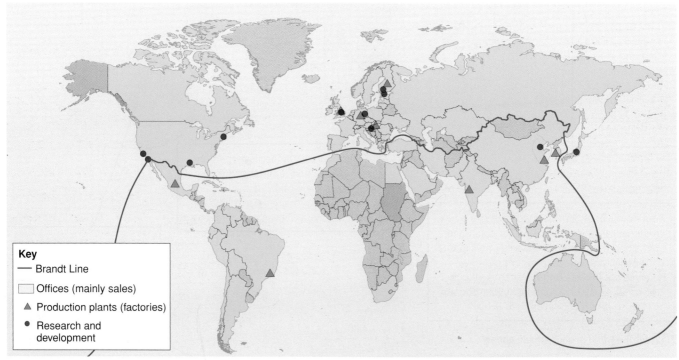

Key

— Brandt Line

☐ Offices (mainly sales)

▲ Production plants (factories)

● Research and development

Figure 5 The global distribution of Nokia's factories, laboratories and offices

Activity

1 Study Figure 5.
   a) Describe the distribution of countries in which Nokia has production plants.
   b) Describe the distribution of countries in which Nokia has R&D laboratories.

Figure 6 Adverts for Nokia and Pepsi (another MNC) in Moscow, Russia

Locating business to minimise costs

MNCs such as Nokia have branches in many countries because they want to reduce costs. With lower costs, their profits are higher. MNCs such as Nokia keep costs low by opening factories and offices in regions of the world that have:

- low labour costs
- cheap land or building costs
- low business rates (the tax paid by a company).

Locating business to be close to the customer

Another reason why Nokia is constantly expanding its range of factories and offices is to be close to its customers, who are spread right across the globe. Nokia's products have massive appeal. Nokia estimates that the mobile phone market had around 2.2 billion people in 2005 and the company expects this to rise to 4 billion in 2009. Growth in mobile phone ownership and subscription has been particularly strong in Less Economically Developed Countries (LEDCs). As consumers in LEDCs have become wealthier, Nokia has expanded its business into Asia, Africa and South America. It has, therefore, opened new sales offices in many LEDCs, located closer to these new customers.

		2003	2004	2005	2006	2007
MEDCs	Finland	22,274	23,069	23,485	23,894	23,015
	UK	1,947	1,903	1,956	2,317	2,618
	USA	6,636	6,706	5,883	5,127	5,269
	Hungary	2,571	3,778	4,186	4,947	6,601
	Germany	3,486	3,522	3,610	3,887	13,926
	Italy	0	0	0	493	2,129
LEDCs	Brazil	1,497	2,640	2,184	1,960	8,527
	China	4,595	4,788	5,860	7,191	12,856
	Mexico	1,290	1,160	1,901	2,764	3,056
	India	184	591	1,609	6,494	11,491

Figure 7 Nokia's employees, 2003–7, in ten largest countries with most employees. Source: Nokia

		2003	2004	2005	2006	2007
MEDCs	USA	4,488	3,430	2,743	2,815	2,124
	UK	2,711	2,269	2,405	2,425	2,574
	Germany	2,297	1,730	1,982	2,060	2,641
	Russia	569	946	1,410	1,518	2,012
	Italy	1,003	884	1,160	1,394	1,792
	Spain	748	768	923	1,139	1,830
LEDCs	China	2,023	2,678	3,403	4,913	5,898
	India	1,064	1,369	2,022	2,713	3,684
	Indonesia	n.d.	n.d.	727	1,069	1,754
	Brazil	n.d.	n.d.	614	1,044	1,257

Figure 8 Nokia's sales, 2003–7 (millions of Euros), in ten countries with most sales. Source: Nokia

Activity

2 Choose two countries, one from each of the following lists:
   MEDCs: Germany, UK, USA
   LEDCs: China, India
   a) Choose a suitable technique to graph the data shown in Figures 7 and 8 for your chosen countries.
   b) Describe the trend shown on each graph.

3 Study Figures 7 and 8. Suggest two alternative reasons for:
   a) the increased sales in LEDCs
   b) the rising employment figures in LEDCs
   c) the falling employment figures in some MEDCs.

4 Study the distribution of Nokia's branches in Figure 5 again. If jobs in R&D are more specialised and highly paid than in other branches, suggest how this distribution:
   a) benefits workers in MEDCs
   b) disadvantages workers in LEDCs.

Figure 9 A Chinese worker tests mobile phones at a production plant in Ningbo, China

What are the benefits of globalisation?

When an MNC such as Nokia opens a new factory or office it can have a positive impact on local people and the local economy. Some jobs are created by the firm itself: Nokia employs 2,000 people in the UK at three sites. This is a direct benefit of the investment made by Nokia in the UK. These new jobs may help to stimulate extra work for other local businesses. This extra work is an indirect benefit of the investment made by the MNC. These benefits to the local economy are known as a positive multiplier.

Different jobs in different locations

Nokia employs a wide range of staff. Some are highly qualified or skilled, such as business managers or R&D staff. Other staff, such as some assembly workers or sales staff, do not require high-level qualifications or as much training. So, like many other MNCs, Nokia has chosen to locate the assembly of basic products in their range in LEDCs where wages are lower.

However, the more highly trained R&D staff tend to work in More Economically Developed Countries (MEDCs). Here, Nokia develops new products, such as hand-held devices capable of filming video, playing games and surfing the web. These devices use the latest technology and therefore need more highly trained staff to develop and produce them. These high-tech products are also aimed at wealthier consumers, usually in MEDCs, so it makes sense to make them in Europe.

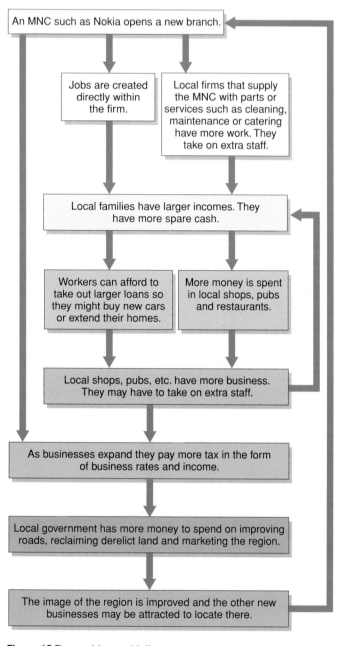

Figure 10 The positive multiplier

Activity

1 Explain the difference between direct and indirect benefits of MNC investment in a new factory or office.

2 Summarise the benefits of the positive multiplier under these headings:
   a) Jobs
   b) Earnings
   c) Spending
   d) Image of the region.

3 Explain why Nokia continues to expand in Africa.

4 Summarise the benefits that Nokia gets from opening new branches in LEDC countries.

The advantages of new technology for Africa

The growth of mobile technology and of MNCs such as Vodacom that provide mobile networks has helped improve communications in some African countries. Many African countries have very few telephone landlines, so rural areas are often cut off. Instead of investing in landlines, countries like Tanzania have used mobile technology to leapfrog the problem. In 2001, Africa became the first region in the world where there are more mobile phone users than people using landlines.

GIS Activity: International Telecommunications Union

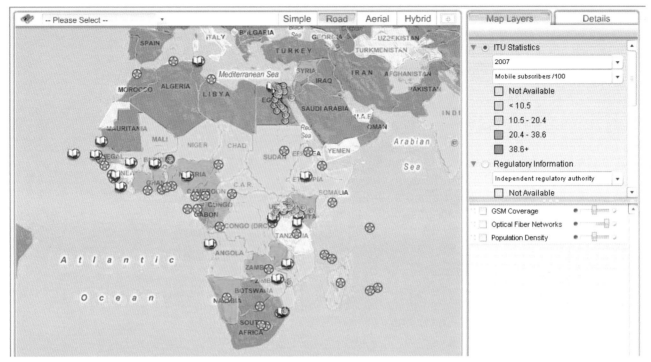

Figure 11 Mobile phone subscribers in Africa. This screenshot is from a GIS (or digital) atlas updated by the International Telecommunications Union. You can use the dialogue box (map layers) on the right of the screen to choose data for different years. The atlas then redraws the map to display the date you have chosen

www.itu.int/ITU-D/connect/gblview/index.html
This weblink takes you to ITU Global View which is the online atlas from which the screenshot in Figure 11 is taken.

Activity

1   Use Figure 11 to describe the distribution of African countries where the number of mobile phone subscribers is
    a)   below 20.4 per 100
    b)   above 38.6 per 100.

2   Use the weblink to view the ITU Global View atlas of Africa. Use the map layers tool to choose '% mobile coverage' and 'broadband subscribers'.
    a)   Describe the patterns on each map.
    b)   How important do you think it is for Africa's development to improve mobile and internet coverage? Explain how these technologies could help:
        i)   African businesses   ii)   African teenagers.

Why do some see globalisation as a threat?

The migration of people between countries for work or study is a major effect of interdependence. Migration has many benefits for the migrant, their family and the countries involved. Many migrants do dirty, dangerous and low-paid jobs that local people do not want to do. Others are highly skilled workers who fill jobs where there are skill shortages, for example doctors and nurses. The UK National Health Service employs thousands of health workers from India and other LEDCs. In fact, more than 11 per cent of all health workers who train in South Asia end up working in the UK.

The brain drain: investigating an ethical issue

In the period 2000 to 2005, a total of between 10,000 and 15,000 newly trained nurses joined the UK National Health Service (NHS) each year from medical schools in LEDCs. The World Health Organization (WHO) estimates that at least 12 per cent of the doctors trained in India now live and work in the UK. This is good for the NHS, which had great difficulty in this period recruiting enough staff from the UK. However, it's not so good for the health service in India and other LEDC countries, which are losing staff in a massive brain drain.

The World Bank estimates that as many as 70,000 of Africa's most highly qualified workers emigrate each year. This may be costing Africa US$4 billion a year. Another estimate suggests that only one-third of medical graduates remain in Ghana each year: the rest leave the country to find better-paid work abroad.

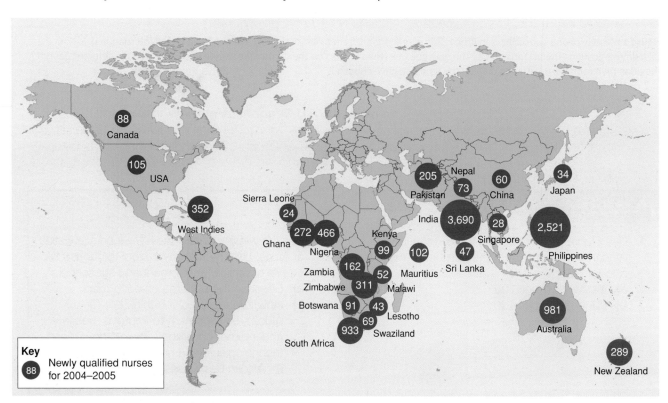

Figure 12 New admissions to the 2004–2005 nursing register who qualified overseas

The costs and benefits of the brain drain from LEDC health services:

- Staff are able to earn many times more than they would do working in hospitals in their home country.
- Staff benefit from training in the latest techniques and treatments.

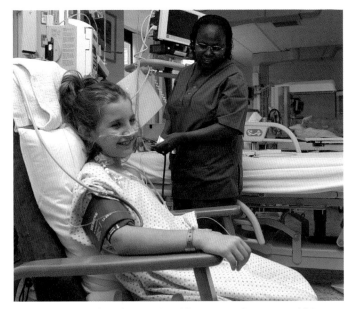

Figure 13 The NHS estimates that 43 per cent of nurses and 31 per cent of doctors starting work in the NHS were trained outside the UK (2005 figures)

- Knowledge of new medical treatments and techniques can benefit the health service in the LEDC if staff eventually return.
- The NHS would have a massive shortage of doctors and nurses if they did not recruit from abroad.
- Waiting times are reduced and patients get faster treatment because staffing levels are kept high.
- Hospitals in Africa are desperately short of trained staff. Morale is low among staff who continue to work long hours for low pay.
- The brain drain means that money spent in an LEDC on university-level education is not converted into a skilled worker who pays tax and who therefore helps to pay for the education of others.

Figure 14 Average annual salaries for Indian health workers in India (2008)

	Rupees	£
GP	190,000	2,369
Nurse	100,000	1,247
Hospital consultant	549,377	6,849
Hospital administrator	206,957	2,580

Activity

1 Use Figure 12. Describe the distribution of countries that supplied more than 100 nurses to the NHS. How many of these countries are LEDCs?

2 Use the internet to research average wages for health staff in the UK. Use a graph to compare your findings with the data in Figure 14.

3 Study the bullet-pointed list of costs and benefits above.
   a) Sort the bullet points into a table using these headings:

	Costs	Benefits
For the British NHS		
For the health service in LEDCs		
For individuals who emigrate from LEDCs to the UK		

   b) Write a 200-word article in which you either strongly support or strongly oppose the migration of health workers from LEDCs.

4 Discuss the concept of globalisation that is illustrated on page 89.
   a) Working with a partner, make a list of any products, brand names, companies, films and music that you associate with each of the following places:
      i) USA   ii) Australia   iii) Japan
      iv) India   v) Africa.
   b) Now combine your list with that of two of your classmates. Discuss your lists.
   c) Do you think that the UK economy relies more on other MEDCs or LEDCs? What are the advantages and disadvantages of this type of interdependence for the UK?

5 Use pages 89–97 to summarise five positive and three negative impacts of greater interdependence.

What are the impacts of globalisation on countries at different levels of development?

What have been the social and economic impacts of the enlargement of the EU?

The European Union (EU) is an example of a **trade bloc**. Every country within the bloc has agreed to trade freely with the other members and also allow free movement of people between their countries. In 2004, the EU was enlarged to include countries from central Europe such as Poland. Unemployment in some of the new member states, such as Poland, was high. Some people warned that a flood of migrants would move to the UK, Spain, Germany and Italy to find work. If they did, would it be a good or a bad thing for the UK and other wealthier members of the EU?

Activity

1 **a)** Use Figure 16 to copy and complete the following:

   The most common reason given by all migrants aged 16–54 was .... whereas the most common reason given by migrants aged 55+ was ....

   b) Suggest how the push and pull factors that cause migration to Spain would be different in each of the following examples:
   i) a wealthy businessman who has just retired in the UK
   ii) a young, single man from Romania who has few qualifications.

2 Use Figure 17 to explain the benefits of migration to the wealthier members of the EU.

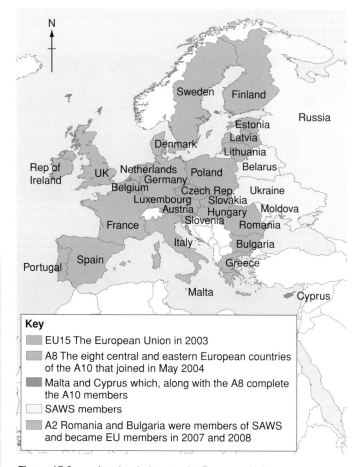

Key
- EU15 The European Union in 2003
- A8 The eight central and eastern European countries of the A10 that joined in May 2004
- Malta and Cyprus which, along with the A8 complete the A10 members
- SAWS members
- A2 Romania and Bulgaria were members of SAWS and became EU members in 2007 and 2008

Figure 15 Countries that belong to the European Union

Reasons	Total	16–54 years	55 years +
Retirement	3.6	0.3	23.3
Joblessness	23.3	25.8	8.8
Seeking a better job	39.0	42.9	15.9
Training or educational reasons	8.4	9.2	3.6
Quality of life	40.0	39.9	40.6
Family reasons (regrouping)	32.1	32.4	30.3
Cost of living	14.3	13.5	19.0
Climate	11.4	7.7	33.0

Figure 16 Reasons for their move given by migrants to Spain

First, many dirty, difficult and dangerous (so-called 3D) jobs are being increasingly shunned by local workers in industrial countries. Second, the current lifestyle of many Europeans is sustained by a wide variety of service jobs – childcare, house cleaning, pizza delivery, etc. – undertaken by foreigners who cannot easily be replaced by locals.

There is still another category of jobs traditionally filled by immigrants, in sectors such as farming, road repairs and construction, hotel, restaurant and other tourism-related services, which, although not completely shunned by local workers, often suffer from seasonal shortages of labour.

Finally, there are several skill and knowledge intensive industries, notably in the fast-moving information technology sector, with an unmet demand for highly skilled immigrants in most industrial countries. There is a scramble for additional skills to develop new technologies, enhance competitiveness and create new jobs.

Figure 17 Extract from an International Migration Organisation publication. World Migration 2005: Costs and Benefits of International Migration

GIS Activity: Eurostat

Using Eurostat to investigate geographical patterns in the EU

http://epp.eurostat.ec.europa.eu

Eurostat is the official website for statistics that cover the members of the EU. Use this weblink to go to the home page. Ensure EN (for English) is selected. Then, on the right of the screen, click on Country Profiles (which has a thumbnail map of the EU) to get to the GIS. Figure 18 is an example of the kind of map you can produce.

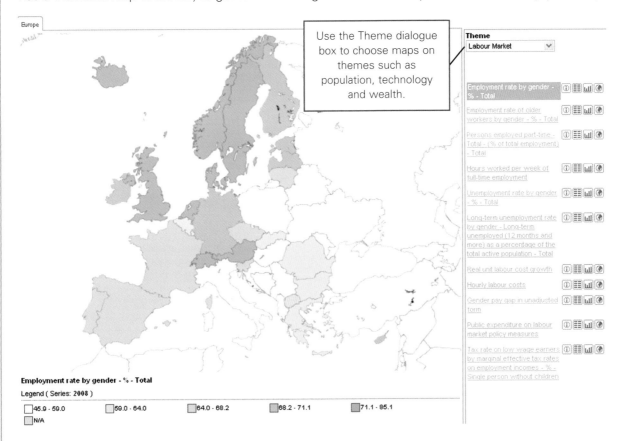

Figure 18 Eurostat website

Activity

1 Use Figure 18.
   a) Describe the distribution of countries where more than 71 per cent of the population (aged 16–64) is in employment.
   b) Compare the map in Figure 18 with Figure 15.
      i) List the countries with less than 64.2 per cent employment.
      ii) Use this map to explain why migration from countries such as Poland and Romania was particularly large after enlargement of the EU.

2 Use the website to investigate the following hypothesis:
   a) internet access is greater in wealthier countries of the EU
   b) intra-EU trade (trade between EU members) benefits the EU15 more than the newer members.

India How have newly industrialised countries such as India and China benefited from globalisation?

Newly industrialised countries such as India and China have benefited from globalisation with economic growth, due to the interdependence in the global economy. Their economies have benefited from recent technological changes and from the interdependence created by flows of people, ideas and investment.

Rank	Forbes 2000 list (2008)	Number of companies
1	USA	598
2	Japan	259
3	United Kingdom	123
4	China (inc. Hong Kong)	109
5	France	67
6	Canada	59
7	Germany	59
8	South Korea	52
9	Australia	51
10	India	48

Rank	Country of birth of resident UK population	Population in thousands
1	India	613
2	Republic of Ireland	420
3	Poland	405
4	Pakistan	377
5	Germany	266
6	Bangladesh	205
7	South Africa	201
8	United States of America	188
9	Jamaica	166
10	Nigeria	140

Foreign investments Indian-owned multi-national companies, like Tata, are very successful in the world economy. In 2008 India was ranked 10th country in the world by Forbes 2000, which lists the location of the world's biggest 2000 companies.

Flows of people Indian migrants work in many other parts of the world, earning money and learning new skills that can be re-invested in the Indian economy. For example, 613,000 people who were born in India currently live and work in the UK.

Improved communication technologies India has excellent universities and good communication networks. It produces thousands of IT and software graduates each year. One example of India's growing demand for consumer items is the rapid growth of mobile phone ownership.

Examples of India's interdependence with the world economy

Flows of ideas and culture The Hindi movie industry based in Mumbai (known as Bollywood) produced 267 films in 2007. These films are extremely popular in South Asia and, with the growth of satellite TV, are now easily accessible in other parts of the world. Their growing popularity led to a stage show, *The Merchants of Bollywood*, which toured successfully in Europe and Australia.

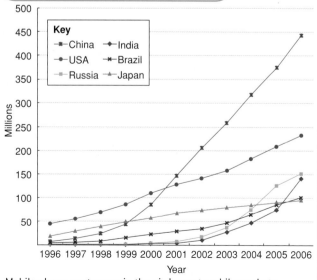

Mobile phone customers in the six largest mobile markets

Ashwini Iyer practises her routine at a rehearsal of the production of *The Merchants of Bollywood* in Maharastra before the show moved to Europe

Figure 19 Examples of India's interdependence with the world economy

How has growing interdependence affected India?

India is the second largest country in the world after China. Its population of 1,132 million people is 17 per cent (or one in six) of the global population. The Indian economy has grown quickly in recent years. As Indians gradually become wealthier they are creating new demand for products. One reason for India's economic growth is due to its interdependence in the global community. Its economy has benefited from recent technological changes and from the interdependence created by flows of people, ideas and investment.

Case study of Tata

Tata is an Indian multi-national company that in 2007–8 earned US$62.5 billion of which 61 per cent was from its business outside India. Tata employs 350,000 people worldwide. It owns a large number of businesses, which include steel makers, car manufacturers, chemicals, energy and a hotel chain. Tata owns 38 companies based in the UK which between them employ a total of 47,000 people. Among the most famous brand names employing UK workers are Jaguar, Land Rover and Tetley Tea.

Early in 2008 Tata announced that it was making the world's cheapest mass-produced car. Called the Tata Nano, this small car is expected to sell for just 120,000 rupees which is only £1,400. Incomes in India are much lower than in the UK. For example, a secondary teacher with less than 10 years' experience earns an average of 128,900 rupees (£1,670) a year. So the announcement of an affordable car was treated with excitement in India where car ownership is low.

Tata plans to keep the production costs for the Nano as low as possible by sourcing its parts from India where labour costs are very cheap. As many as 97 per cent of the components used in the car will be provided by European multi-national companies who have factories in India. In 2008, about 2 million cars were produced in India but none are as cheap as the Nano.

Activity

1 Outline how India benefits from greater interdependence.

2 Use Figure 19.
   a) Compare the rise in mobile phone ownership in India and China.
   b) Compare mobile phone ownership in India and Japan.
   c) The population in China is only slightly larger than India. Japan has a population of only 127 million. Predict how the mobile phone market might change in the future in these three countries?

3 Using Figure 19 for ideas, create a display for your classroom that shows how India is connected to the rest of the world. You should include at least one map or graph. You could also use a search engine to find images of Indian products and brand names.

The windscreen will be supplied by the French company Saint-Gobain Sekurit. This firm employs 200,000 people in 56 different countries

Steel for the body parts will be supplied by Tata and Ispat which are both Indian companies

Behr, another German firm, will supply the heating and ventilation systems. They employ 19,500 people including 1,710 in Asia

The German company Bosch will supply the computer that controls the engine. Bosch employ 271,300 people and over half of these work outside Germany

The seatbelts will be supplied by Autoliv which is a Swedish company. Autoliv employ 41,900 people in 32 countries

The steering system will be supplied by ZF which is another German company employing 60,000 people in 119 plants in 25 countries. ZF steering systems are used in many famous cars including:

| VW Tiguan | Jaguar | Volvo V70 | Ford Mondeo |

Flag indicates ownership of company. Each car may be made in a different country eg Jaguar is made in the UK

Figure 20 The new Tata Nano that will sell for around £1,400   101

What are the advantages and disadvantages of the growth of Tata?

Some groups in India oppose the growth of global companies like Tata and have protested against the Nano and plans to build a new factory. The Nano was going to be built in Singur, West Bengal. Twenty of the firms who supply parts for the car were also going to build new factories here. Between them they would have created hundreds of skilled and semi-skilled jobs in this poor region. The local government supported the new development, but after violent opposition in the summer of 2008, Tata decided to pull out. The car is now likely to be built in Maharastra state in western India.

Ratan Tata, Chairman of Tata Motors

I decided to build the Tata Nano some years ago when I observed families riding on two wheelers, the father driving a scooter, his young kid standing in front of him, his wife sitting behind him holding a baby. Surely these families deserve a safe, affordable, all-weather form of transport. A vehicle that could be affordable and low cost enough to be within everyone's reach. Built to meet all safety standards, be low in pollution and high in fuel efficiency.

India's cities are already congested with cars, buses and auto-rickshaws. A cheap car will be very popular and will add substantially to the congestion problem. Exhaust emissions will cause air quality to fall leading to even more health problems for poor people in our cities.

Indian environmentalist

I protested against the decision to build the Tata factory here along with over 15,000 other people. Three quarters of local people are farmers: we have no experience of working in factories. We argued that the loss of our land would have led to hunger and malnutrition. The state government offered some compensation but it wasn't enough. Women like me would have been worst affected. I have no legal papers for my smallholding so I wouldn't have got any compensation at all.

Farm labourer from West Bengal

Tata will produce about 250,000 Nanos per year at first. Demand for the Nano from other developing countries will be huge so Tata expect production to expand to 1 million cars a year. Some of these will be built in India and the rest in other LEDCs. The European companies that are providing the parts are excited about the prospect of their business expanding into more LEDC car markets.

Chairman of Bosch

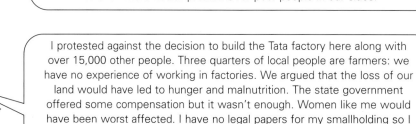

Figure 21 The advantages and disadvantages of growth at Tata

Activity

1 How might the Tata Nano benefit lower income families?

2 Suggest the possible effect of the Tata Nano on:
   a) India's city streets
   b) levels of pollution in Indian cities.

3 a) Use Figure 21 to explain why some of the people in West Bengal object to the Tata Nano factory.

   b) Use the case study of Tata to complete the following table.

Benefits for India created by Tata's success	Problems for India created by Tata's success
Economic	
Environmental	
Social	

Improving your extended writing

Extended answers are marked using a levels marking scheme. These work in a very different way from a points marking scheme and require a different approach in your answer. You need to make sure that your answer covers the breadth of the topic, but a good answer also needs depth by including specific knowledge and/or case study material. This is where your revision notes are vital to success. Your answer to the extended writing question will often determine whether you achieve the top A/A* grades.

Mark Scheme

Level One – Answer demonstrates a superficial understanding of the concept of globalisation. The candidate may make simple statements identifying jobs and an improved standard of living as benefits.

Level Two – Answer demonstrates an understanding of the concept of globalisation. Answer may begin to describe improvements in standards of living and outline a multiplier effect where the extra wealth created is used to improve services such as schools.

Level Three – Answer demonstrates a clear understanding of the concept of globalisation. Answer may describe a multiplier effect where wealth created is used to improve services such as schools and the infrastructure of the country. Answer should contain examples and specific knowledge.

Sample question

Explain how globalisation (greater interdependence) has benefited the people who live in India. [6]

Student answer for Candidate A

The people will have more job opportunities as companies from the West enter India. This gives the people and the government more money, which makes them wealthier. This means the government can build new facilities such as schools and hospitals. This will improve the lifestyles of the people living in India. Globalisation has made India better known as more countries rely on India for such things as trade and information.

What the examiner has to say!

It is the quality of the answer that will gain marks in this question not the number of points made. In this answer the candidate demonstrates a clear understanding of the concept of globalisation. However there is no specific knowledge and the answer lacks depth. This is a good level two answer worth 4 marks.

Student answer for Candidate B

There have been vast amounts of foreign investment in India in recent years. Many trans-national companies have located in India and produced many jobs, e.g. Coca Cola alone employ 24,000 people in India. The global market has also led to India having its own TNCs such as Tata producing a wide range of products from telecommunications to clothing. Therefore there has been an increase in wealth and standard of living that has led to huge advances in the quality of roads, harbours and airports because the TNCs need to transport their goods worldwide. The increase in wealth has also led to improvements in the education and the health system which means that the future for India looks good.

What the examiner has to say!

This is a good quality answer that demonstrates a clear understanding and contains specific knowledge and examples. This is a level three answer worth at least 5 and probably 6 marks.

Exam practice

1 Describe how globalisation has benefited the people who live in the UK. [6]
2 Explain why the world is more interdependent today than it was in the past. [6]
3 Explain why there has been a growth in the number and size of trans-national companies (TNCs) in recent years. [6]

India

Foreign investment in India

Coca-Cola first opened a bottling plant in India in 1993. Coca-Cola invested US$1,000 million in their Indian business between 1993 and 2003. In 2008 the company employed 6,000 people in India. They claim that a further 125,000 people have indirectly benefited from such jobs as distribution (i.e. lorry drivers who deliver the bottles).

Coca-Cola is one of many foreign owned multi-nationals that have invested in India in recent years. These investments are further examples of interdependence because money spent by, in this case, an American company is creating jobs in a different part of the world. However, some Indian protest groups are unhappy with the way in which big businesses operate. They claim that big business ignores the needs of poorer communities and disadvantaged groups (like the farmers in West Bengal who would have lost their jobs had Tata built its new factory). In the case of Coca-Cola there have been numerous protests against the soft drinks firm. Most protests have been by local people who claim that their wells are running dry as the drinks company takes water out of the ground for production of the cola. Some have also complained about pollution from the factories. Coca-Cola deny that they have caused any such problems and are trying hard to win over local people by getting involved in local community aid projects.

key location

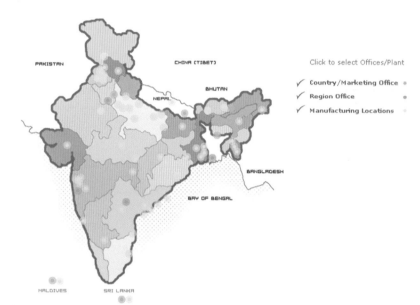

Figure 22 Map of Coca-Cola plants in South Asia

Figure 23 Local people protesting about falling water levels in their wells after Coca-Cola opened a bottling plant in Kerala, India

www.coca-colaindia.com
This is the site of Coca-Cola India. The site has information about its management of water. Read both sides of the issue and make up your own mind where you stand.

Campaign to Hold Coca-Cola Accountable
Coca-Cola Crisis in India

Communities across India are under assault from Coca-Cola practices in the country. A pattern has emerged as a result of Coca-Cola's bottling operations in India.

- Communities across India living around Coca-Cola's bottling plants are experiencing severe water shortages, directly as a result of Coca-Cola's massive extraction of water from the common groundwater resource. The wells have run dry and the hand water-pumps do not work any more. Studies, including one by the Central Ground Water Board in India, have confirmed the significant depletion of the water table.

- When the water is extracted from the common groundwater resource by digging deeper, the water smells and tastes strange. Coca-Cola has been indiscriminately discharging its waste water into the fields around its plant and sometimes into rivers, including the Ganges, in the area. The result has been that the groundwater has been polluted as well as the soil. Public health authorities have posted signs around wells and hand pumps advising the community that the water is unfit for human consumption.

- In two communities, Plachimada and Mehdiganj, Coca-Cola was distributing its solid waste to farmers in the area as 'fertilizer'. Tests conducted by the BBC found cadmium and lead in the waste, effectively making the waste toxic. Coca-Cola stopped the practice of distributing its toxic waste only when ordered to do so by the state government.

- Tests conducted by a variety of agencies, including the government of India, confirmed that Coca-Cola products contained high levels of pesticides, and as a result, the Parliament of India has banned the sale of Coca-Cola in its cafeteria. However, Coca-Cola not only continues to sell drinks laced with poisons in India (that could never be sold in the US and EU), it is also introducing new products in the Indian market. And as if selling drinks with DDT and other pesticides to Indians was not enough, one of Coca-Cola's latest bottling facilities to open in India, in Ballia, is located in an area with a severe contamination of arsenic in its groundwater.

Figure 24 Web extract from India Resource Centre – an organisation that campaigns on behalf of local communities against big companies

Activity

1 Describe the distribution of Coca-Cola manufacturing locations in India.

2 Suggest what benefits are created by foreign multi-nationals locating in India for:
   a) local people
   b) the multi-national company.

3 Outline three different objections that Indian communities have had with local bottling plants.

4 From what you have learned about Tata and Coca-Cola, summarise the advantages and disadvantages of interdependence for India.

Before you finish eating breakfast this morning, you've depended on more than half the world.

Figure 25 Martin Luther King, the black American civil rights campaigner

How have patterns of trade hindered economic progress in the least developed countries?

Speaking in the 1960s, Martin Luther King (Figure 25) reminds us that countries rely on each other for the goods and services that we all need for our daily lives. Since then, faster aircraft, larger ships, and the use of standard-sized containers for moving goods around the world have all contributed to making us rely even more on trade with other countries for our everyday needs.

Goods produced in one country and then sold abroad are **exports.** The goods that a country buys from abroad are **imports.** Countries also buy and sell services.

Comparing the UK and Ghana's trade

Shop in the local supermarket and you can buy a chocolate bar made from cocoa beans grown in Ghana. Ghana doesn't make much chocolate, but it does export a lot of beans and the European Union is its biggest customer. At the same time, people shopping in the supermarkets of Accra, Ghana's capital city, can buy tinned tomatoes or frozen chicken produced in the European Union. Ghana and the European Union trade with each other but, of course, they both trade with a lot of other countries as well.

Ghana imports a lot of manufactured goods whereas a lot of Ghana's exports are raw materials that haven't been processed – like cocoa beans. The UK, by comparison, exports a huge range of different processed and manufactured goods.

Activity

1 Discuss Figure 25 with a partner. What do you think Martin Luther King meant?
   a) Make a list of all the things you have used by breakfast.
   b) Suggest which countries might export these items to the UK.
   c) Using the internet, research the main exporters of breakfast items such as coffee, tea and fresh orange juice.

2 Use Figure 26. Compare Ghana's trade with that of the UK. Pick out the main similarities and differences using connectives:

   whereas   similarly   on the other hand

3 Use the evidence in Figure 27 to explain the advantage of quotas and subsidies for:
   a) consumers in Europe
   b) farmers and businesses in Europe.

4 Explain the likely effect of:
   a) the EU shoe quota for workers in Vietnam
   b) the import of cheap food for farmers in Ghana.

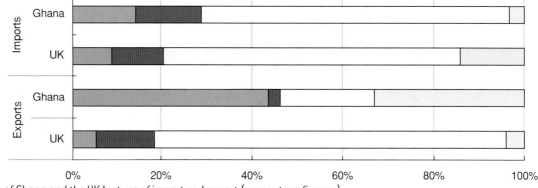

Figure 26 Comparing the trade of Ghana and the UK by type of import and export (percentage figures)

Should trade be free and uncontrolled?

Free trade, or trade that takes place without any limits or control, is the aim of many countries. The advantage of free trade is that a country can export as many goods as it wants to its trade partners. This is good for the farmers and businesses who produce the exported goods and services. The disadvantage of free trade is that a country can find itself swamped by cheap imports made in countries that have lower labour costs. These cheap imports are good for consumers, but could cause jobs to be lost in similar industries within the importing country. To avoid this problem some countries protect themselves from cheap products. They can do this in one of three ways:

- Placing quotas that restrict the amount of these imported goods each year.
- Placing an import duty or tax on the imports to make them more expensive.
- Paying a subsidy to its own farmers and businesses so that their goods can be sold at a lower price to consumers.

The current international pattern of trade is a mixture of free trade and protected trade. This causes problems for both More Economically Developed Countries (MEDCs) and Less Economically Developed Countries (LEDCs). Figure 27 summarises three of these problems.

Farmers in the EU receive government subsidy to keep the cost of production low so that food is cheap for consumers in Europe. Some of this food is then exported to Africa.

The EU imports billions of pairs of shoe from China and Vietnam. Half of the 2.5 million pairs of shoes sold in the EU we made in China.

EUROPEAN UNION

CHINA

GHANA

Local farmers find it hard to sell their own tomatoes on this market in Accra, Ghana. Imports of frozen chicken, rice and tinned tomatoes (subsidised in the EU) are cheaper than local food.

In 2006, the EU placed a quota to restr the number of shoes imported from Asi into Europe. It did this to protect the job of 850,000 people working in shoe manufacturing in Italy and elsewhere in the EU. However, the effect on low-paic workers in China and Vietnam could be disastrous.

Ghana's second most important source of foreign exchange comes from the export of cocoa beans. Most are sold to chocolate manufacturers in Europe and the USA.

Prices for primary commodities such as cocoa fluctuate up and down, making it hard for cocoa farmers to plan the growth of their business or even earn a decent wage. The average wage for a cocoa farmer in Ghana is just £160 a year.

Figure 27 The problems created by the international pattern of trade

Trade blocs

Trade is made easier where partnerships have been agreed between countries. These trading partnerships are known as trade blocs. The European Union (EU) is one example of several trade blocs that exist around the world. Figure 28 shows two more. Each country within each bloc already has a free trade agreement with other countries in the bloc, or is working towards a free trade agreement. For example,

China already has free trade agreements with some members of the Asia-Pacific Economic Co-operation (APEC) and is working towards similar partnerships with the other LEDC members of the group by 2010. However, it has no free trade partnership with the UK or with the EU. That is why the EU is able to impose the quota on imports of Chinese shoes described in Figure 27.

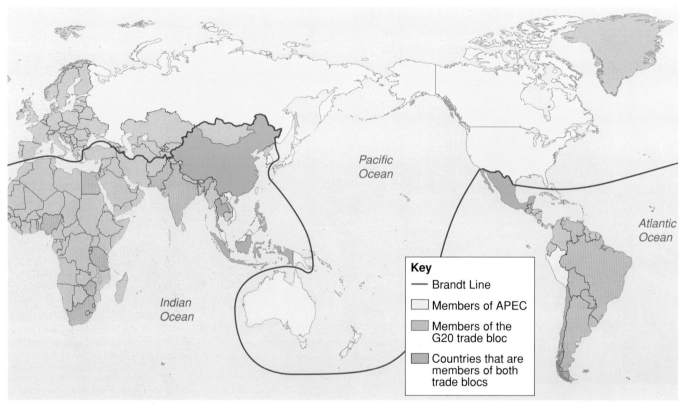

Figure 28 Trade blocs: APEC and G20

Activity

1 Use Figure 28.
   a) Describe the distribution of APEC countries.
   b) Compare the distribution of APEC countries with that of G20 countries.

2 Explain the advantage of free trade for the LEDC countries in the G20 trade bloc.

Ghana | Case study of Ghana and its trade

Figure 29 Joyce Oppong Kyekyeku and her daughter Doris breed chickens for a living but they are competing against cheaper imported chickens from Europe. The Ghanaian government imposed tariffs on the imports but was forced to drop them by the International Monetary Fund

Ghana's main exports are gold, cocoa and timber. These are all **primary commodities** – raw materials that have not been processed. Ghana's imports include oil (another primary commodity) plus machinery, tools, vehicles and medical equipment – all **manufactured goods**. Ghana also earns money from abroad by attracting foreign tourists; we say that this is another way in which Ghana earns **foreign exchange**.

Like all countries, Ghana needs to trade successfully in order to create wealth and jobs. However, Ghana faces a number of problems with the international pattern of trade.

Ghana is not a member of any of the major trade blocs. For this reason it cannot rely on free trade with other countries. One of its main exports is cocoa beans. For years this product has had a relatively small tariff when it enters the EU: buyers have paid 3 per cent tax. However, the EU tariff on imports of processed cocoa products was much higher. For example, buyers of cocoa butter paid a 7.7 per cent import tax. This tariff was in place to protect the chocolate manufacturers in the EU from cheap imports of cocoa products. It made it very hard for manufacturers in Ghana to sell their cocoa products in Europe and so discouraged the growth of manufacturing.

However, things are at last beginning to improve for Ghana. In 2007 Ghana signed an Economic Partnership Agreement (EPA) with the EU. This guarantees it zero or lower tariffs on most of its exports to the EU until 2022. This includes a zero tariff on both cocoa beans and cocoa butter. So Ghana's cocoa farmers and chocolate manufacturers can now experience free trade.

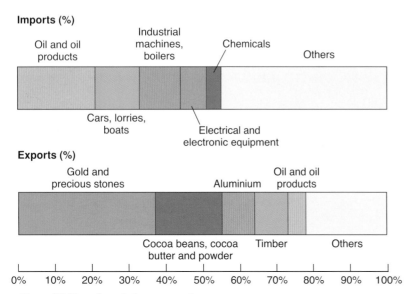

Imports (%)

Oil and oil products | Industrial machines, boilers | Chemicals | Others

Cars, lorries, boats | Electrical and electronic equipment

Exports (%)

Gold and precious stones | Aluminium | Oil and oil products

Cocoa beans, cocoa butter and powder | Timber | Others

0%   10%   20%   30%   40%   50%   60%   70%   80%   90%   100%

Figure 30 Ghana's main imports and exports

Another problem that Ghana experiences with trade is that food imported from the EU is sold so cheaply that it undercuts the cost of locally grown food. Imports of rice, chicken and tinned tomatoes are particularly cheap because the EU has subsidised the farmers who produce these goods. Any that cannot be sold in Europe are then sold cheaply in Africa: a practice known as dumping. Ghana tried to place import tariffs on these items but was forced to drop them as a condition of its loan from the World Bank.

MAKE TRADE FAIR

Figure 31 The Make Trade Fair logo was launched by Oxfam in 2002. Oxfam is a Non-Governmental Organisation (NGO) that is drawing attention to the dumping of subsidised products in LEDCs

www.oxfam.org/en/campaigns/trade
This is the homepage of the Oxfam Trade Campaign. You'll find explanations of why the current pattern of international trade is unfair for LEDCs.

Figure 32 Michael Stipe of the band REM has milk dumped on him to draw attention to the Make Trade Fair campaign. EU milk subsidies mean that European cows 'earn' US$2 a day, which is more than the daily income of a Ghanaian farmer

Activity

1   Use Figure 30 to complete the following description of Ghana's pattern of trade:

   Ghana's largest export is … at 37 per cent, followed by cocoa beans which make up … per cent of Ghana's exports. Oil is the largest single import which makes up … per cent of all imports.

2   Which of Ghana's imports/exports are:
   a) primary commodities
   b) manufactured or processed goods?

3   Explain why Ghana would benefit from joining a trade bloc such as the G20.

4   Suggest how Ghana could benefit from the Make Trade Fair campaign.

5   Design a poster or leaflet featuring information about Ghana and headed 'Make Trade Fair for Ghana'.

How are global patterns of development identified?

What do we mean by development?

One common view of development is that it can be measured economically: that increasing wealth or decreasing levels of poverty are indicators of development. We will start by considering whether or not this is helpful.

Development is...

- reducing levels of poverty
- increasing levels of wealth
- reducing the gap between the richest and poorest members of society
- creating equal status for men and women
- creating justice, freedom of speech and political participation for everyone
- ensuring that everyone is safe from conflict and terrorism
- ensuring that everyone fulfils their basic needs: food, water and shelter
- ensuring that all children have good standards of education.

Figure 1 Different ways of seeing development

Figure 2 Development is ...

Figure 3 Development is ...

Activity

1   Study Figure 1. Work in pairs to discuss this list.
    a) What are the advantages and disadvantages of each of these statements as a definition of development?
    b) Choose the five statements that you think give the best definition of development. Join with another pair and justify your choice.
    c) Working in a team of four, produce a joint statement that defines development. Each member of the team must contribute and agree with the statement.

2   Working on your own, explain which aspects of human development are illustrated by Figures 2 and 3. Write a caption for each figure.

Using national wealth as a measure of development

The wealth of a country is usually measured by its Gross National Product (GNP) per person. The GNP per person of a country is calculated by:

Step 1 Add up the total value of goods and services produced by people living in that country and by people abroad who are still citizens of that country.

Step 2 Divide this figure by the total number of citizens of that country.

This gives a figure which can be thought of as the average annual income for a citizen of that country. Helpfully, the World Bank and United Nations (UN) now refer to GNP as Gross National Income (GNI) per person. So for example, the average annual income (GNI or GNP) in Mali, Africa, is US$350 (or about US$1 a day). Remember, this is an average, so some people earn more than this and others earn less. In fact, 73 per cent of Mali's population earns less than US$1 a day.

Figure 4 shows the 1980 Brandt Line which divides countries into one of two categories: More Economically Developed Countries (MEDCs) to the North and Less Economically Developed Countries (LEDCs) to the South. It is also coloured to show GNP. The World Bank divides the countries of the world into four categories defined by GNP. It describes these as high income, upper middle income, lower middle income and low income countries. For the details of this classification check the details shown in the key to Figures 4 and 5.

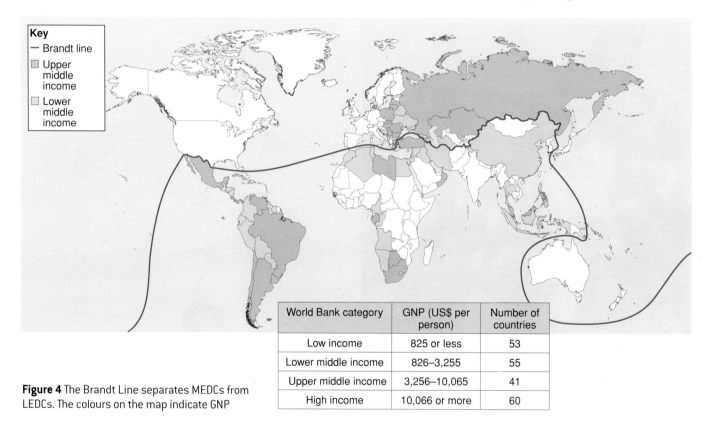

Key
— Brandt line
▨ Upper middle income
▢ Lower middle income

World Bank category	GNP (US$ per person)	Number of countries
Low income	825 or less	53
Lower middle income	826–3,255	55
Upper middle income	3,256–10,065	41
High income	10,066 or more	60

Figure 4 The Brandt Line separates MEDCs from LEDCs. The colours on the map indicate GNP

The Brandt Line

Public awareness of the development gap is not new. It was first brought into the news headlines in the Brandt Report in 1980. This report, by Willy Brandt, a German politician, drew a line on the map that separated the richer countries from the poorer ones. This map was developed to separate the More Economically Developed Countries (MEDCs) from the Less Economically Developed Countries (LEDCs). As you can see on Figure 5, the MEDCs are situated mainly in the northern hemisphere. The LEDCs are mainly in the tropics and southern hemisphere. The line loops around Australia and New Zealand to include them in the richer half of the map. This famous map draws attention to the gap between the richer North and the poorer South and is still in use today. But is it still relevant and accurate?

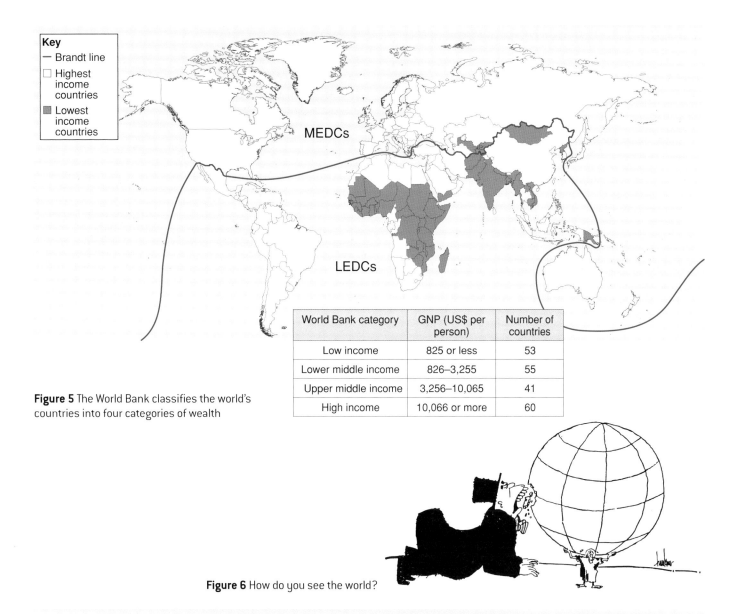

Key
— Brandt line
☐ Highest income countries
▦ Lowest income countries

MEDCs

LEDCs

World Bank category	GNP (US$ per person)	Number of countries
Low income	825 or less	53
Lower middle income	826–3,255	55
Upper middle income	3,256–10,065	41
High income	10,066 or more	60

Figure 5 The World Bank classifies the world's countries into four categories of wealth

Figure 6 How do you see the world?

Activity

1 Discuss the cartoon, Figure 6.
  a) Describe each character: how they are dressed and what they are doing?
  b) Who do the two figures represent?
  c) Explain the actions of the larger figure.

2 Use Figure 5.
  a) Describe the distribution of higher income countries.
  b) Describe the distribution of lowest income countries.

3 Study Figure 4.
  a) Describe the distribution of :
    i) lower middle income countries
    ii) upper middle income countries.

b) Identify countries that have:
    i) an upper middle income but are south of the Brandt Line
    ii) a lower middle income but are north of the Brandt Line.

4 Study Figures 4 and 5.
  Which do you find more helpful: the two categories of the Brandt Line or the four categories defined by the World Bank?
  a) Suggest the advantages and disadvantages of each system.
  b) Do you think there is an argument to re-draw the Brandt Line? If so, where should it go?

Using health data as an indication of development

Health data is also often used to describe a country's level of development. Two commonly used indicators are:

- **infant mortality rate (IMR)** – the number of children who die before the age of one for every 1,000 that are born. This figure varies widely, from 270 in Sierra Leone to only three in Sweden.
- average life expectancy – the average age to which people can expect to live.

	Under-5 mortality rate		Infant mortality rate (under 1)	
	1960	**2006**	**1960**	**2006**
Sub-Saharan Africa	278	160	165	95
Middle East and North Africa	249	46	157	36
South Asia	244	83	148	62
East Asia and Pacific	208	29	137	23
Latin America and Caribbean	153	27	102	24
Russia and the countries of eastern Europe	112	27	83	24

Figure 7 Improving health care has cut infant mortality

Activity

1 Study Figure 7.
   a) Copy the following statement:

   The lowest infant mortality rate (IMR) in 2006 was in .... In this region IMR improved from ... per 1,000 in 1960 to ... per 1,000 in 2006. The highest IMR in 2006 is in the region of ....

   b) Choose a style of graph to show the improvements made by any one region in the table.

2 Make a copy of Figure 8. Working with a partner, suggest how you could complete the blank spaces in the table.

Why use health data?

A number of factors contribute to improved life expectancy and lower IMR. Increased government spending on health care, clean water and sanitation (sewage disposal) will all have an impact on health data. That's why this data is a useful indication of development. Around 17 million people die every year from infectious diseases such as HIV/AIDS, malaria and tuberculosis. Of these, 90 per cent are people living in LEDCs and many of these are children. Many of these deaths are preventable: improving the quality of water and providing mosquito nets would be very low-cost measures to achieve this.

	High life expectancy and low IMR might indicate that ...	Low life expectancy and high IMR might indicate that ...
Government spending on hospitals and clinics	a wealthy government is able to prioritise health spending	
Government spending on preventive medicine (e.g. immunisation)		lack of training facilities might result in too few medical staff
Diet		
Access to safe drinking water	most people have access to clean water in their homes	
State of sanitation		many people live in shanty housing with no proper sewage system
Standards of personal and social education in schools		

Figure 8 What health data may be telling us about a country's development

Changes to average life expectancy

Between 1960 and 2007, life expectancy increased in most countries of the world. Some of the biggest improvements were in LEDCs. For example, average life expectancy in South Asia leapt from 48 to 64 years. However, due to HIV/AIDS average life expectancy decreased in 21 countries during the 1990s. All but one of these countries is in Africa. In Zimbabwe, the average life expectancy fell by a staggering 22 years from 55 to 33.

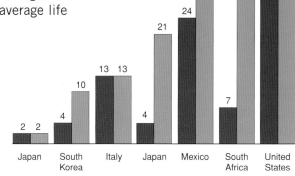

Figure 9 Percentage of adults who are obese in selected countries

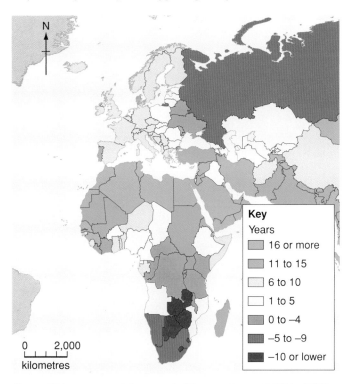

Figure 10 Increase and decrease in life expectancy, 1960 to 2003

How will the ageing population affect our health?

In MEDCs primary health care is generally very good and people have long life expectancy. However, the cause of death is often influenced by people's choice of lifestyle. Over-eating, lack of exercise and alcohol/drug addiction often contribute to the cause of death. For example, poor diet and lack of exercise can lead to weight gain and then to obesity. Obesity increases the risk of a number of long-term (or chronic) health problems. It increases the risk of stroke, heart disease and can also lead to Type 2 diabetes. A recent report in the UK predicts that by 2050:

- 60 per cent of adult men in the UK will be obese
- 50 per cent of adult women will be obese
- 25 per cent of all children under 16 will be obese
- the current cost to the NHS of treating people who are ill because they are overweight will double from £5 billion to £10 billion a year
- the cost to society and business (through, for example, days lost from work due to ill health) will rise to £49.9 billion by 2050.

Activity

3 Study Figure 9. Describe the distribution of countries which have the most improved life expectancy.

4 Suggest why life expectancy has increased in some countries more than others.

5 **a)** Explain why people in wealthy MEDCs do not always have healthy diets.
   b) Explain what effect these diets might have on health data.

6 **a)** Do some research into the main causes of death in MEDCs and LEDCs.
   b) Choose one major cause of death that is easily preventable in LEDCs and explain how this issue could be solved.

7 Produce a poster or PowerPoint presentation. Use your poster or presentation to show:
   a) how our lifestyle decisions can affect our health; or
   b) how the cause of death varies from one country to another; or
   c) how rising levels of obesity will have negative impacts on the UK's future.

Ghana

What are the regional patterns of development in Ghana?

Ghana is a country in sub-Saharan West Africa. Poverty and hunger are both problems in Ghana. The Gross National Income is $520 per person and 45 per cent of the population live on less than $1 a day (UN latest figure for 2005). Around 55 per cent of the working population work on farms, usually as smallholders or landless labourers. These labourers are among Ghana's poorest earners and earn so little they usually have no savings. When food is in short supply the price at the market goes up, so it's perhaps not surprising that 19 per cent of Ghanaian children under 5 are malnourished.

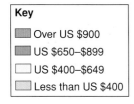

Key
- Over US $900
- US $650–$899
- US $400–$649
- Less than US $400

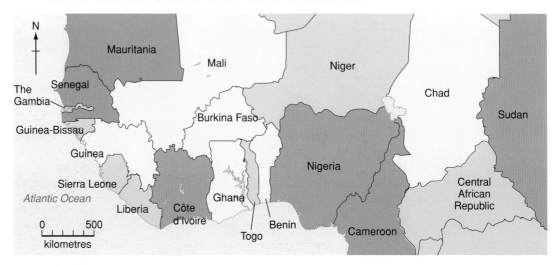

Figure 11 Gross National Income (GNI) per person 2008 for the countries of West Africa

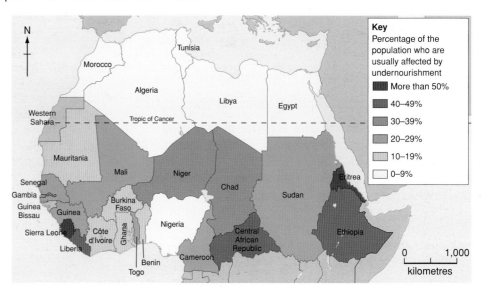

Key
Percentage of the population who are usually affected by undernourishment
- More than 50%
- 40–49%
- 30–39%
- 20–29%
- 10–19%
- 0–9%

Figure 12 Percentage of the population who are normally affected by undernourishment

Activity

1 Use Figure 11 to describe the distribution of the poorest countries in this region.

2 **a)** Compare Figures 11 and 12. What evidence is there that the poorest countries are also those with the most undernourished population?

b) Explain why the children of a landless labourer in Ghana are at more risk of malnourishment than the children of someone with regular pay in an office job.

Ghana has a tropical climate. In the southern regions of the country, the long wet season means that farmers can grow food crops like sorghum, or cash crops like cocoa. Almost 90 per cent of Ghana's crop is grown on tiny farms by 2.5 million smallholders. However, the average cocoa farmer only earns about £160 a year.

The price of cocoa goes up and down on the world market. It's difficult to make a profit and invest it in the farm. Further north the annual rainfall is much lower and it can be unreliable. This means that the land has to be used less intensively and farmers here can grow fewer food crops. Instead they keep a few goats.

Figure 13 A cocoa farmer lays out cocoa beans on giant tables made of rush matting to dry in the intense Ghanaian sun. After six days they will have developed a full flavour

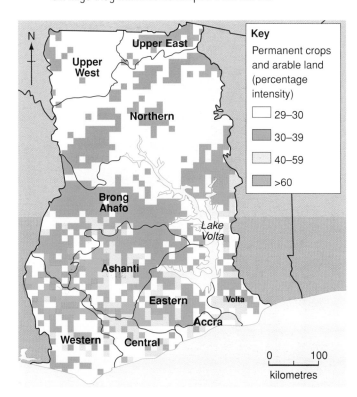

Figure 14 Where crops are grown in Ghana

Key
Permanent crops and arable land (percentage intensity)
- 29–30
- 30–39
- 40–59
- >60

Activity

3 Use Figure 14.
   a) List the four regions of Ghana that have most permanent crop land.
   b) Which regions have least crop land?
   c) Suggest how this map might help explain regional patterns of poverty and hunger.

4 Use an atlas (or the internet) to research patterns of rainfall in Ghana. Use this information to explain the pattern of permanent crop land in Figure 14.

5 Use the internet to research fair trade for cocoa farmers. Produce a poster explaining how fair trade supports farmers and their wider communities.

A north–south divide

Ghana suffers from a sharp north–south divide. Northern Ghana is very rural whereas the south of the country is more urban. Incomes in the more urban southern regions of the country are 2.4 times higher than in the rural north. The reasons for this include:

- the south has better transport so industry has grown faster there
- the south is more accessible to tourists and has benefited from the growth of tourism during the 1990s
- the north has unreliable patterns of rainfall that make farming more difficult than in the south.

Activity

1 Describe the distribution of regions in Ghana where average incomes were:
   a) above $200 in 2000
   b) below $200 in 2000.

2 Using evidence from Figures 14 and 15 describe and explain which parts of Ghana are likely to have the highest rates of malnutrition.

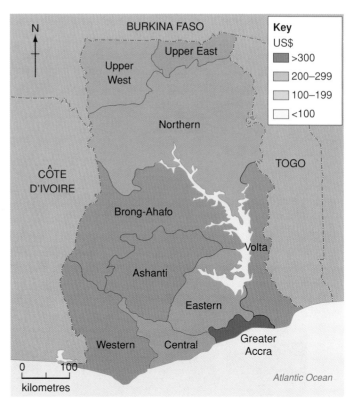

Figure 15 The regional pattern of income in Ghana (2000 survey)

Figure 16 Village life in rural Ghana

The northern regions of Ghana face severe problems such as poverty, lack of job opportunities (especially for women) and lack of safe drinking water. The region has a harsh climate and farming is an unreliable way of making a living. The lack of decent roads and public transport make it difficult for rural families to get to local towns to visit friends, go to the shops, or to get medical attention. There is a severe shortage of teachers in the northern regions of Ghana. In rural northern Ghana, the Infant Mortality Rate (IMR) is twice as high as in urban areas of the south. Malaria, acute respiratory infections, diarrhoea, malnutrition and measles are still the five main causes of death in young children.

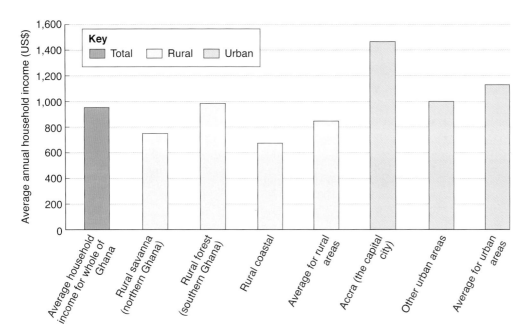

Figure 17 Average household incomes in urban and rural parts of Ghana (2000 survey)

Region	Percentage access to health services	Percentage of child malnutrition	
		1998	2003
Western	46.9	24.4	36.9
Central	67.2	22.9	31.5
Greater Accra	80.9	9.1	40.4
Volta	49.5	22.2	30.1
Eastern	60.1	24.7	32.9
Ashanti	69.0	25.9	46.6
Brong Ahafo	53.8	22.2	26.1
Northern	35.0	48.6	33.9
Upper East	26.7	54.1	32.6
Upper West	30.4	44.4	24.8
National average	57.6	26.0	35.8

Figure 18 Regional patterns of human development in Ghana

Activity

3 Use Figure 17 to compare the average household incomes:
 a) in Accra with those in other urban areas
 b) in Accra with rural areas in the north.

4 Suggest how each of the following factors contributes to the high infant mortality rates in the north of Ghana:
 a) poor transport networks
 b) low family incomes.

5 Use the data in Figures 15, 17 and 18 to produce a short presentation or poster about the regional patterns of development in Ghana. Your presentation should include:
 a) a description of the regions in which development is lowest and highest
 b) an annotated map or graph.
 c) suggestions for an aid agency: outline the main development challenges facing one poor region of Ghana.

What progress is being made towards achieving the Millennium Development Goals?

The United Nations (UN) is an international organisation supported by 192 different countries. One of the UN's aims is to encourage and assist human development. In 2000, the UN set eight development targets known as the **Millennium Development Goals (MDGs).** The goals use data to measure the development of every country since 1990. The challenge is to meet all of the goals by 2015. The MDGs are described in Figure 19.

1 End extreme poverty and hunger:
- Halve the number of people living on less than a dollar a day.
- Halve the number who suffer from hunger.

2 Achieve universal primary education:
- Ensure that all boys and girls complete a full course of primary schooling.

3 Promote gender equality:
- Make it easier for girls as well as boys to access primary and secondary education.

4 Reduce child mortality:
- Reduce by two-thirds the number of children who die before their fifth birthday.

5 Improve health for mothers:
- Reduce by three-quarters the number of women who die in childbirth.

6 Combat AIDS, malaria and other diseases:
- Halt and begin to reverse the spread of these killer diseases.

7 Ensure environmental sustainability:
- Protect the environment, so that future generations can continue to benefit from it.
- Halve the number of people without access to clean water.
- Improve life for 100 million people who live in shanty towns by 2020.

8 Build global partnerships for development:
- Make improvements to aid.
- Boost freedom, justice and democracy.
- Make it easier for the poorest people to have access to medicines.
- Cancel some debts and reduce others.
- Make world trade fairer.

Activity

1 Use Figure 20.
   a) What was the under fives' mortality rate in sub-Saharan Africa in:
      i) 1990?
      ii) 2006?
      iii) What is the target?
   b) What was the ratio of girls to boys in secondary education in South Asia in:
      i) 1990?
      ii) 2006?
      iii) What is the target?
   c) Which regions are most likely to:
      i) reach both goals?
      ii) fail to reach both goals?
      iii) reach only one goal?

Figure 19 The eight Millennium Development Goals

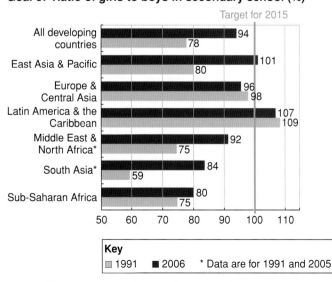

Goal 3: Ratio of girls to boys in secondary school (%)

Key
■ 1991 ■ 2006 * Data are for 1991 and 2005

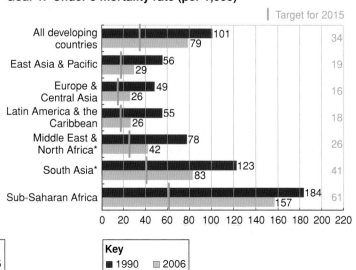

Goal 4: Under 5 mortality rate (per 1,000)

Key
■ 1990 ■ 2006

Figure 20 Progress towards goals 3 and 4 MDGs

GIS Activity: World Bank

http://devdata.worldbank.org/atlas-mdg

This interactive world map allows you to check on the progress made towards the MDGs of regions or countries.

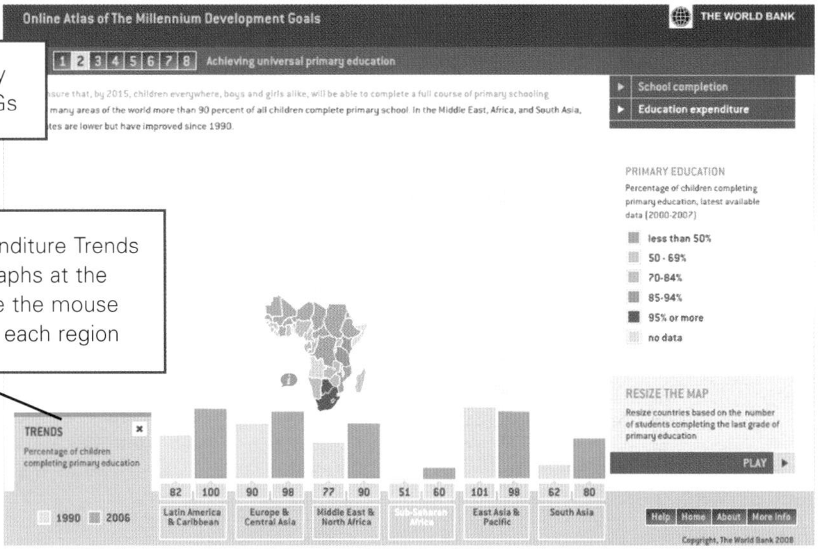

Click on each Goal button to display maps that relate to each of the MDGs

Click on the Completion/Expenditure Trends button to reveal the bar graphs at the bottom of the screen. Move the mouse over the screen to highlight each region

Figure 21 A screenshot showing progress towards MDG 2. Percentage of children completing primary education

Move the mouse over the map to name each country and display its data. Clicking on the country reveals further data.

Use the zoom feature to zoom in and out

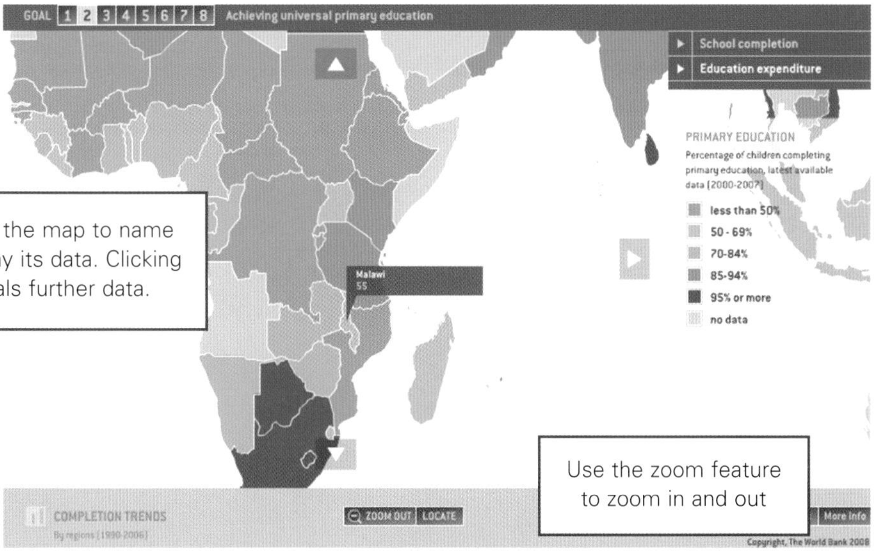

Figure 22 A screenshot showing a zoomed in view of sub-Saharan Africa

Activity

1 a) Describe the distribution of countries in Africa that have:
  i) less than 50 per cent
  ii) more than 95 per cent
  of children completing primary education
b) Suggest why this is a useful measure of a country's development.

2 a) Use this GIS site to investigate global patterns of:
  i) child mortality
  ii) immunisation
  iii) maternal (mother) mortality.
b) What are the similarities and differences in these patterns?

Progress towards Goals 2 and 3

In MEDCs most children attend school and most adults can read and write. Most EU countries have 100 per cent primary enrolment and 100 per cent adult literacy. However, not all children in LEDCs are able to go to primary school. It is estimated that 115 million primary school aged children did not attend school in 2002 and nearly all of these were in LEDCs. Things are gradually improving. By 2006 this number had fallen to 93 million and by 2008 it had fallen again to 75 million. The reason why so many children still miss school is poverty. Poor families often cannot afford to send all of their children to school – which is not necessarily free. Children are expected to help support the family by doing an informal job and earning some money. Daughters are sometimes kept off school to help look after younger brothers and sisters or to do household chores such as fetching water or firewood. Of the 75 million children who missed primary school in 2008, well over half were girls.

Why is it particularly important to improve education for girls?

The fact that lots of girls miss school means that in many LEDCs adult literacy is lower in women than in men. This difference between men and women is an example of **gender inequality** and it has serious consequences. For example:

* the child of an uneducated mother is twice as likely to die before the age of one as a child whose mother had a full education
* women who are well educated tend to marry later and have smaller families
* education (especially at secondary and university level) empowers women, i.e. it gives them a higher status and better chances in life.

The UN has set MDGs to improve primary education and reduce gender inequality. Achieving universal primary education would mean that every child has the opportunity to enrol and complete a primary school education. Promoting gender equality and empowering women means increasing the number of teenage girls in education.

	1990		2004	
	Male	Female	Male	Female
Sub-Saharan Africa	60	40	69	53
Middle East and North Africa	66	39	74	52
South Asia	59	34	66	42
East Asia and Pacific	88	72	93	81
Latin America and Caribbean	87	83	90	88
Russia and the countries of Eastern Europe	98	94	98	95

Figure 23 Improvements in adult literacy rate from 1990 to 2004 (%)

Activity

1 Explain why some poor parents do not send all of their children to primary school.

2 Explain why adult literacy is not useful for describing differences between the countries of the EU.

3 Study Figure 23.
   a) Copy and complete the following statement:

   The lowest adult literacy in 2003 was in .... In this region female literacy improved from .... per cent in 1960 to .... per cent in 2004. Male literacy improved from .... per cent to .... per cent in the same period.

   b) Choose a style of graph that shows the improvements made by any one region in Figure 23.

4 Use Figure 23 to identify those regions that:
   a) have made the greatest developments in education
   b) face the greatest challenges of gender inequality.

Figure 24 The advantages of better education for girls

Figure 25 Schoolgirls taking part in a youth radio programme in Botswana

Activity

5 Use Figure 24 to extend the explanation of each of the following statements:
An educated mother …
- **spots the early signs of ill health in her child so …**
- **understands the importance of a balanced diet so …**
- **recognises the importance of a full education for her daughter so …**

Examiner's Tips

Understanding command words

Explain is a common command word in the GCSE geography examination. The examiner is looking for evidence that you understand the complexity of the issue. A simple statement will only get one mark. To get a better mark you will need to elaborate on your explanation. So, to get a good mark you need to ask yourself the 'So what … ?' question. The question and answers below show how this works.

Sample question

Study Figure 25. Explain how an educated girl can improve the standard of living of her family in later life. [4]

Student answer for Candidate A

Education is good for young women because it means they will have some qualifications.✓ Also they are more likely to give their own children a healthy diet.✓

What the examiner has to say!

This is a reasonable answer but it is worth only 2 marks. The student has made two simple statements but there is no elaboration. After the first sentence the student should have asked themselves 'So what … ?' They could have gone on to say that 'qualifications would enable the woman to get a better paid job so she would no longer be living in poverty and no longer rely on her children to help support the family. This means she would choose to have a smaller family than if she were poor.' This elaboration of the first sentence would get the student 2 more marks.

Student answer for Candidate B

An educated girl will want a good job and a career so she will marry later✓ and have fewer children.✓ This means that she will not need to rely on her children to help support the family income✓ so her children will complete their own education.✓ Another benefit of education is that an educated young mother knows how to provide a healthy diet for her children✓ so they will grow up in good health and with a much lower chance of malnutrition.✓

What the examiner has to say!

This is an excellent answer which is worth 4 out of 4. The student gives two reasons and each one is fully elaborated.

Mali

Who is helping countries reach their MDGs?

Working towards the MDGs is a major concern for many people working in government and in the voluntary sector. A disaster like the Sichuan earthquake (page 54) is instantly reported around the world on the internet and by satellite. This often creates enormous public sympathy and people from both rich and poor countries give generously to provide **emergency aid**. However, emergency aid is only a small part of the aid given by both governments and Non-Government Organisations (NGOs) such as OXFAM, ActionAid or Christian Aid. Most aid is, in fact, planned over long periods of time to tackle poverty and improve quality of life. This is known as long-term, or **development aid**. It is these long-term projects, supported by both governments and NGOs, that address the MDGs.

Oxfam is one of many Non-Government Organisations (NGOs) that provide long-term development aid to Niger and Mali. In one of their projects they are working with ADESAH, a local NGO, to support primary schools for the children of **pastoral farmers** who live in the border area between western Niger and northern Mali. This nomadic community of cattle and goat herders is very poor. Many families do not feel they can afford to send their children to school, especially girls. The project supports 48 primary schools. Its successes include:

- 4,053 pupils enrolled in school (2004), including 1,818 girls (44.85 per cent)

- women are heavily involved in the management of the schools and participate physically and financially in the payment of children's school fees and in the canteen

- the ratio of pupils to books has improved from one book for five pupils to two books for three pupils.

Figure 26 Class in Taboye school, Mali, which has received support from Oxfam and the local NGO ADESAH. It's an MDG to ensure that all boys and girls in the world complete their primary education

Millennium Development Goal 2: DFID's aid to education

Globally, there are some 75 million primary-aged children not enrolled in school – 55 per cent (41 million) of whom are girls (UNESCO Institute of Statistics, 2008). This lack of basic education deprives young people of choices and opportunities, and makes it harder for countries in the developing world to tackle poverty and disease.

Sub-Saharan Africa accounts for more out-of-school children than any other region: 35 million, including 19 million girls (UIS). Meanwhile, across South and West Asia 18 million primary-aged children are out of school, 10 million of them girls (UIS).

But progress is being made. Global enrolment in primary education increased by over 41 million between 1999 and 2005. There are now 95 girls enrolled in school for every 100 boys, compared with 92 girls for every 100 boys in 1999. The number of primary-aged children not enrolled in school fell by over 28 million between 1999 and 2006.

DFID is spending £8.5 billion pounds over ten years to ensure that, by 2015, children everywhere, boys and girls alike, will be able to complete at least five years of quality education. Most of the money will be going to sub-Saharan Africa and South Asia.

We are working closely with the governments of poor countries to improve both the access to and the quality of schooling.

Although it's a tough target, the achievements of some countries do give grounds for optimism. In countries like Uganda and Malawi, for example, the number of children enrolling in primary school has doubled in five years and is now over 90 per cent.

Figure 27 A web extract from the UK's Department for International Development (DFID).

How well is South Asia progressing?

South Asia has the lowest rate of female literacy among all regions with only 63 per cent of young women and 46 per cent of adult women being able to read and write. The number of girls enrolling in secondary school has improved but is not equal to the number of boys.

The number of children missing from primary school in India was 25 million in 2003.

India's college/university system is one of the largest in the world with over 10 million students.

The number of children missing from primary school in India in 2007 was 9.6 million.

Only 1 in 10 young people go into higher education. Most of these are from well-off families.

Less than 40 per cent of Indian teenagers attend secondary schools.

A survey in the late 1990s found that 72 per cent of schools in India did not have a library.

The curriculum needs to change so that students become independent learners and critical thinkers.

Parents are often unwilling to send teenage daughters to school where there are no female teachers.

Indian universities produce the third largest number of engineers each year.

Rural children often have to travel long distances to secondary school. The cost of travel prevents many poor families from sending their children to school.

Figure 28 Education in India: progress or not?

Activity

1 Read the description of the aid projects in Figure 26.
   a) Describe who is providing this aid.
   b) Give three details that describe the group who benefit from this project.
   c) Give two facts that could be used as a measure of success of the project.
   d) Explain how this project should empower women.

2 Use Figure 27.
   a) Describe who is providing this aid.
   b) Name the two regions that are identified as having most children out of school.

3 Produce a poster or presentation that summarises the information in Figure 28 under two headings:
   a) Development challenges (outlining the problems facing children today).
   b) Progress (outlining the progress towards reaching MDG 2 on education).

4 a) Sort the facts in Figure 28 into two: positive statements and statements that indicate more progress is needed.
   b) Use these statements to suggest:
      i) three reasons why Indian schools are not fully attended
      ii) three strategies for improving school attendance.

MDG 6 Combating HIV

Millennium Development Goal 6 has set the target of reversing the spread of HIV, malaria and other diseases by 2015. These diseases result in an early death for millions of people. They are also a major cause of poverty in many communities. HIV most commonly infects people of working age. Deaths among the work force not only cause distress for families but also reduce the earning power of the family.

Sub-Saharan Africa is the region of the world that has been hardest hit by HIV, an incurable disease that attacks the immune system and which eventually leads to AIDS. In 2007, it is estimated that 1.5 million sub-Saharan Africans died of AIDS and more than 11 million AIDS orphans were living in these African countries.

There are signs that this MDG might reach its target in at least some African countries. Rates of infection from HIV reached a peak in the late 1990s. Since then, in most countries of sub-Saharan Africa, the percentage of adults who are living with the virus has levelled out or fallen. This is because fewer people are becoming infected because of the success of education programmes. In Uganda, for example, HIV infection rates fell when the government introduced a programme of training for health care workers and education and counselling for the public.

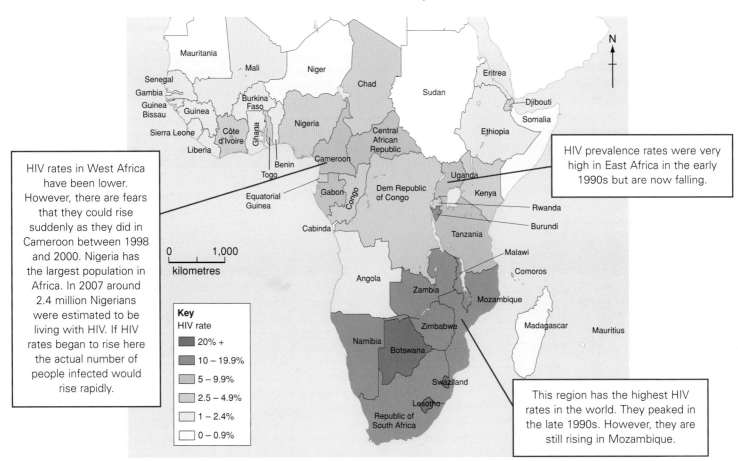

Figure 29 HIV prevalence rate (2007) in sub-Saharan Africa (percentage of adults aged 15–49 who are HIV positive)

Activity

1   Use Figure 29 to describe the distribution of countries with an HIV prevalence rate:
    a) below 2.5 per cent
    b) higher than 10 per cent
    c) higher than 20 per cent.

2   Explain why a slight increase in HIV infections in Nigeria would cause concern.

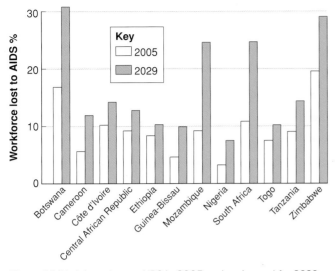

Figure 30 Workforce lost to AIDS in 2005 and estimated for 2029

Activity

3 Explain the links between HIV/AIDS and poverty. Use Figures 30 and 31 to provide evidence for your explanation.

4 a) Choose a suitable graphical technique to process the data in Figure 32.
   b) Describe the trends shown on your graphs.
   c) Use your graphs and Figure 29 to compare trends in East Africa and Southern Africa.
   d) Use your graph to predict what could happen to each country by 2015.

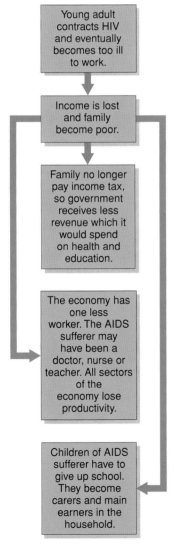

Figure 31 The social and economic consequences of HIV

	Malawi	Mozambique	Uganda	Lesotho	Nigeria	Ghana	South Africa
1990	2.1	1.4	13.7	0.8	0.7	0.1	0.8
1991	3.6	1.8	13.8	1.5	1.0	0.1	1.2
1992	5.6	2.3	13.5	3.1	1.2	0.3	1.9
1993	8.0	2.9	13.1	5.7	1.5	0.7	2.9
1994	10.3	3.7	12.5	9.7	1.9	1.3	4.4
1995	12.1	4.5	11.8	14.2	2.2	1.8	6.2
1996	13.1	5.5	11.1	18.3	2.5	2.2	8.4
1997	13.7	6.5	10.5	21.1	2.7	2.4	10.6
1998	13.8	7.6	9.8	22.8	2.9	2.5	12.8
1999	13.7	8.6	9.1	23.6	3.0	2.4	14.5
2000	13.5	9.5	8.5	23.9	3.1	2.4	15.9
2001	13.3	10.3	7.9	23.9	3.2	2.3	16.9
2002	13.0	11.0	7.4	23.8	3.2	2.2	17.6
2003	12.8	11.5	6.9	23.7	3.2	2.2	17.9
2004	12.5	11.9	6.5	23.6	3.2	2.1	18.1
2005	12.3	12.2	6.1	23.4	3.2	2.0	18.2
2006	12.1	12.3	5.7	23.3	3.1	2.0	18.2
2007	11.9	12.5	5.4	23.2	3.1	1.9	18.1

Figure 32 Trends in HIV prevalence rates (1990–2007)

MDG 7 Improving water supply in sub-Saharan Africa

The UN has set the target of halving the number of people that do not have access to clean water and **sanitation** (the safe disposal of sewage) by 2015. To meet this target we could:

- waste less water by fixing leaks
- use water more efficiently, for example, by using grey water (waste water from washing) to water the garden
- increase the amount of freshwater supplies.

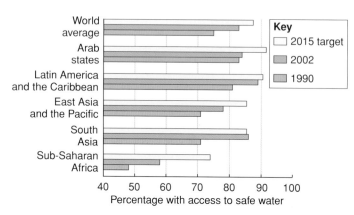

Figure 33 Will each region achieve its Millennium Development Goal for safe water?

Activity

1 **a)** Working with a partner, make a list of all the ways that you use water every day.
   b) How many of these uses are essential and how many could you live without?

2 **a)** Study Figure 33. Which regions are:
   i) likely to reach their target?
   ii) unlikely to reach their target?
   b) Discuss why we need to set these targets.

3 Produce a 400-word newspaper article explaining:
   a) why we need to achieve the Millennium Development Goal for water and sanitation
   b) how we could achieve it.

GIS Activity: Millennium Development Goals (MDG) website

www.mdgmonitor.org

This website allows you to plot progress towards the Millennium Development Goals. Click on 'MDG map' to view the map below.

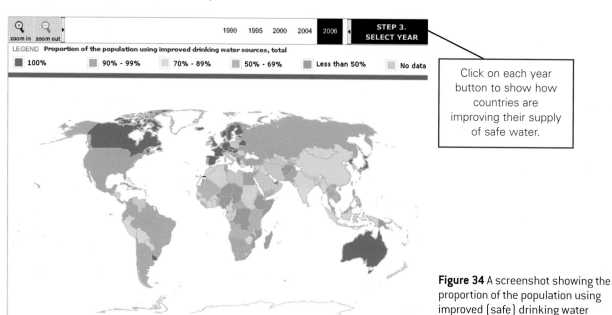

Click on each year button to show how countries are improving their supply of safe water.

Figure 34 A screenshot showing the proportion of the population using improved (safe) drinking water

South Africa   Improving the water supply to Johannesburg, South Africa

In sub-Saharan Africa, people living in urban areas are twice as likely to have access to water as people living in rural areas. In the **informal settlements** of Africa's cities many people do not have access to piped water. They are forced to buy water from private sellers off the back of carts. As a result, people who live in cities in LEDCs can pay up to 50 times the amount for water as people who live in cities in MEDCs.

In 1986, South Africa reached an agreement with its neighbouring country, Lesotho, to provide water to the city of Johannesburg. The resulting Lesotho Highlands Water Project (LHWP) is a massive scheme. It involves the construction of six major dams in Lesotho and 200 km of tunnel systems to transfer water to the Vaal River system in South Africa. The River Vaal then carries the water into Gauteng Province and to the city of Johannesburg.

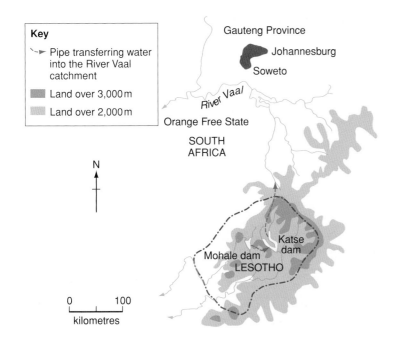

Figure 35 A map of the LHWP water management and transfer scheme

What are the advantages and disadvantages of the LHWP?

Lesotho is one of the world's poorest countries. Its Gross National Income per person is US$590, it has an unemployment rate of around 50 per cent and no natural resources to sell except water. The Lesotho government is hoping that the LHWP will help to develop the country. The income received from selling water through the LHWP is providing 75 per cent of the country's income.

The project is predicted to cost US$8 billion, which is being given on loan from the World Bank. The South African government will eventually have to pay this money back. The Lesotho government will receive income for the sale of its water. In the long term this could help Lesotho develop its own water management schemes.

In the short term Lesotho is still struggling with water shortages and poor sanitation. Local people have not had access to any of the water supplied by the dams since all of the water is being piped to South Africa.

But the percentage of people with a safe water supply in South Africa increased from 83 per cent to 87 per cent between 1990 and 2002. In 2002 only 76 per cent of people in Lesotho had a safe water supply and only 37 per cent had sanitation.

Most of the LHWP water is being transferred to Johannesburg in the Gauteng province of South Africa. But many residents of Johannesburg are angry because their water bills increased before receiving the improved water service. Some of these people did not even have access to basic water resources. Bills went up to fund the dam and to pay for repairs to leaking pipes.

Local people launched a campaign to halt the construction of the Mohale dam until the water pipes in Johannesburg improved. In 2000 up to 50 per cent of water was simply being wasted through leaking pipes. Despite this, construction of the Mohale dam continued ahead of schedule.

The dams will provide hydro-electric power (HEP) as well as water. The Muela dam is connected to a 72 megawatt hydro-electric power station that is providing a renewable source of cheap electricity for Lesotho. Lesotho is also benefiting from improved roads which were constructed to gain access to the dam sites.

However, many people have been displaced by the construction of the dams and the flooding of the reservoirs. The Katse dam, the first major dam of the project, completed in 1998, affected more than 20,000 people. Many of these people were relocated and given compensation but they claim the money they received was too late. They were also given training so that they could find new jobs, but the training has been criticised and most of the displaced people are still in low-income jobs.

New job opportunities have been created working on the construction of the project. About 20,000 people have moved into informal settlements to work on the dams. However, this has led to a massive increase in AIDS, prostitution and alcoholism.

The project has also destroyed thousands of hectares of grazing and arable land. Since only 9 per cent of Lesotho is considered arable, this could lead to huge problems in the nation's food supply.

The project will affect the flow of water downstream of the dams. As well as a decrease in the amount of water, it is thought that the dams will reduce the amount of sediment, oxygen levels, nutrients and even the temperature of the water. This will have negative impacts on people, wetland habitats and wildlife, including many endangered species.

Figure 36 The Mohale dam. You can see this dam on Google Earth: reference location: 29 27′ 29.97″S, 28 5′56.17″E

River	Senqunyane
Capacity	958 million m³
Height	145 m
Material	A concrete-faced embankment filled with 7.8 million m³ of rock
Interconnecting tunnel	To Katse (32 km long)
Water transfer capacity	10.1 m³ per second
Initial loan	US$45 million (funded to Lesotho and to be repaid to the World Bank by South Africa)
Number of affected people	7,400, many of whom lost their homes

Figure 37 Factfile on the Mohale dam (completed 2002)

Activity

1 Summarise the aims of the Lesotho Highlands Water Project.

2 Use the text on these pages to complete a copy of the following table. You should find more to write in some boxes than in others.

	Short-term advantages (+) and disadvantages (−) of LHWP	Long-term advantages (+) and disadvantages (−) of LHWP
Lesotho	+	+
	−	−
South Africa	+	+
	−	−

3 Summarise what each of the following groups of people might think about the LHWP:
   a) a farmer in the Lesotho Highlands
   b) a government minister in Lesotho
   c) residents in Johannesburg.

4 Do you think the LHWP is an example of a good, sustainable water management project? Explain your reasons.

Activity

5 Choose five techniques shown in Figure 38. For each technique explain how it either collects rainwater or recharges groundwater.

6 Explain why this type of management is sustainable.

Are there alternative ways to manage South Africa's water?

South Africa has 539 large dams, which is almost half of all the dams in Africa. But despite this, there are still a large number of South Africans without access to clean drinking water. Many of these people live in rural, remote parts of South Africa; they are too isolated to become part of the big projects such as the LHWP and they are too poor to drill boreholes to tap into groundwater supplies. Instead they have to rely on cheap, small-scale methods of rainwater harvesting.

A case study of sustainable water management on a small farm

Ma Tshepo Khumbane is a South African farmer who teaches rainwater harvesting techniques. Her management strategies are affordable and practical for families, no matter how small the farm is or how little money they have.

Rainwater harvesting can be carried out by individual households or involve whole communities. These methods of water management are not usually big enough to have negative impacts on the surrounding drainage basin so they are sustainable. They use ways that are cheap, practical and easy to maintain using appropriate technology. A number of these techniques are shown in Figure 38; they are designed to:

- collect and use rainwater, for example, by collecting water from the roof of the farm
- maintain soil moisture by encouraging as much infiltration as possible; in this way groundwater stores are recharged.

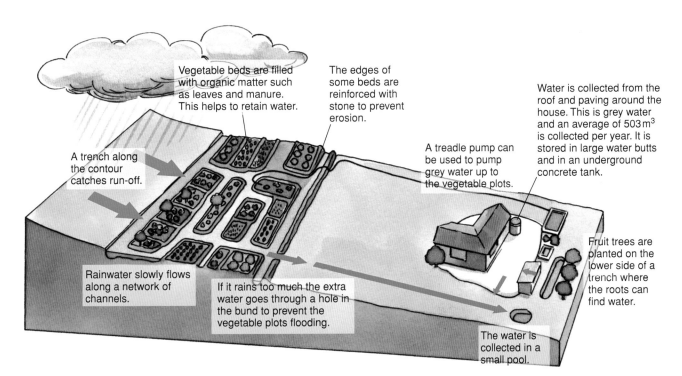

Figure 38 Rainwater harvesting techniques used by Ma Tshepo Khumbane

The village of Athol in Limpopo province is one community to have benefited from the teachings of Ma Tshepo Khumbane. In 1982 the community was struggling with drought and malnutrition. Despite having no regular access to water, the villagers of Athol have learned to manage their water sustainably by collecting rainwater and maintaining soil moisture. The villagers' next aim is to build a small stone dam to collect and store rainwater; this will provide a more secure water supply. They are appealing to the government to provide tractors to speed up the process.

Appropriate technology

In South Africa most water is drawn from wells using hand pumps. This can be hard work for women and children. In the 1970s and 1980s money was invested in diesel pumps. These pumps abstract water much more quickly, but they are expensive to install and maintain. An engineer has to service the pump regularly and parts can be expensive.

Now there is an alternative to hand pumps and diesel pumps that is more appropriate to the level of technology and wealth in poorer sub-Saharan African communities. A company has invented a children's roundabout that pumps water out of a borehole. It is called a PlayPump® water system. The children play on the roundabout and save their mothers a lot of work! There are now more than 1,200 PlayPump® systems located in South Africa, Zambia, Mozambique, Swaziland and Lesotho.

A PlayPump water system costs US$14,000. Advertising on the billboards that surround the

Figure 39 Ma Tshepo Khumbane inspects vegetables growing in an earth basin. The good soil in the middle of each basin collects rainwater

storage tank are available for rental and the income that is generated covers the cost of maintenance for the system. PlayPump® systems such as the one at the Thabong nursery school in Davieton (Figure 40) are increasing access to clean drinking water, are sustainable, and should have no long-term negative effects on the environment.

Activity

1 Compare the effects of diesel pumps with the effects of hand pumps.

2 Explain the advantages of the new roundabout pumps.

3 Explain why this water management technique is more appropriate for poor communities than a diesel pump.

Figure 40 Roundabout waterpump at the Thabong nursery school in Davieton

Glossary

A

Aftershock – An earthquake that occurs minutes or days after a major earthquake. Aftershocks are usually smaller than the first, large earthquake but can cause the collapse of weakened buildings so are still a hazard.

Ash – Powdered rock fragments thrown from a volcano during an explosive eruption.

B

Biofuel – Fuel used in transport or for heating homes that is made from plant material instead of fossil fuel (oil).

Braided – A river pattern made when a shallow river has deposited gravel islands so that the river is split into several smaller channels. From above the river looks a little like plaited (or braided) hair.

C

Caldera – A huge hollow in the earth's surface caused by the collapse of a volcano after a massive eruption.

Carbon neutral – A product or development (such as a housing estate) that does not add any extra carbon dioxide emissions to the atmosphere over its lifetime.

Cinder cone – A volcanic hill that is conical in shape. A cinder cone is formed by the eruption of red hot lava that is thrown from the vent. The globs of lava are full of gas bubbles. They solidify to form pebble sized fragments of rock that have the texture of honeycomb.

Climate – Taking **weather** readings over long periods of time, and then working out averages, patterns and trends.

Commute – When people who live in rural areas travel every day to jobs in urban areas.

Constructive plate margin – Where two plates are pulling apart and new crust is created.

Counter urbanisation – The movement of people and businesses from large cities to smaller towns and rural areas.

Crust – The outer layer of the Earth which is made of solid rock. There are two different types of crust. The crust under the oceans is very dense but only about 10–12km thick. The continents are made of rocks that are less dense. The continental crust is an average of 35km thick but much thicker than this where there are mountains.

D

Deformation – The process of bending and folding the crust. Deformation is caused by plate movement.

Deposition – The laying down of material in the landscape. Deposition occurs when the force that was carrying the sediment is reduced.

Desertification – When the **climate** of a dry region becomes even drier. Vegetation dies or is eaten by grazing animals and the soil becomes vulnerable to soil **erosion**.

Destructive plate margin – Where two plates meet and one is destroyed as it is pulled under the other.

Development aid – Help which is given to tackle poverty and improve **quality of life**. Development aid is usually given to combat long-term problems such as improving education or health care rather than to deal with an emergency such as a famine.

E

Economic migrant – A migrant who moves in order to find work.

Emergency aid – Help that is given urgently after a natural disaster or a conflict to protect the lives of the survivors.

Endemic – A disease that is constantly present or a threat in a certain geographical area or amongst a specific group of people. For example, malaria is endemic in many parts of sub-Saharan Africa, including Malawi.

Enhanced greenhouse effect – A strengthening of the greenhouse effect caused by the release by humans of large concentrations of **greenhouse gases** into the atmosphere.

Erosion – The wearing away of the landscape.

Exports – The sale of products from one country to another.

F

Floodplain – The flat area beside a river channel that is covered in water during a flood event.

Fold mountains – Large mountain ranges that have been formed by folding as two tectonic plates collide into one another. The largest fold mountains in the world are the Himalaya. These are formed by the collision of the Indian plate into the rest of Asia. It is estimated that India is moving northwards at about 50mm per year.

Foreign exchange – The way in which countries earn money from abroad (for example, by the sale of **exports** or by attracting foreign tourists).

Glossary

G

Gender inequality – Differences in income or **quality of life** that exist between men and women.

Geothermal energy – Energy produced by pumping water into hot rocks. The hot water can be used to heat buildings by passing it through radiators. In other places the rocks turn the water to steam. The steam is then used to turn a turbine so that electricity is generated.

Glacials – Cold periods in Earth's history when glaciers have advanced and ice sheets increased in size.

Global warming – The slight rise in average temperature of the Earth's atmosphere that is a sign of **climate** change.

Globalisation – Flows of people, ideas, money and goods are making an increasingly complex global web that links people and places from distant continents together.

Gorge – A steep sided, narrow valley. Gorges are often found below a waterfall.

Greenhouse gases – Gases such as carbon dioxide and methane that are able to trap heat in the atmosphere.

Groundwater flow – The flow of water through rocks.

H

Hard engineering – Artificial structures such as sea walls or concrete river embankments. They are constructed to try to control a natural process such as a river flood or coastal erosion.

I

Impermeable – Soil or rock which does not allow water to pass through it, such as clay.

Imports – The purchase of goods from another country.

Infant Mortality Rate (IMR) – The number of children who die before the age of one for every 1000 that are born.

Infiltrate – The movement of water from the ground surface into the soil.

Informal settlement – Homes where the householders have no legal rights to the land, that is, they do not have legal housing tenure. Informal settlements are commonly known as shanty towns and squatter settlements.

Interglacials – Warmer periods in Earth's history when glaciers have retreated and ice sheets have decreased in size.

Island arc – A group of islands formed by the eruption of volcanoes. When viewed from space the islands make a crescent (or arc) shape in the sea.

J

Jökulhaup – An Icelandic word that means 'glacial outburst'. This is a sudden flood that is caused by the eruption of a volcano under the ice.

K

Kyoto Protocol – An agreement made by world leaders in Kyoto, Japan, to begin to reduce carbon dioxide emissions.

L

Lag time – The difference in time between a rain storm and the peak flow of floodwater (the maximum discharge) down a river.

Lahar – An Indonesian word that describes a flood of water and volcanic ash or a mudslide down the slope of a volcano. Lahars are caused when rainwater mixes with loose volcanic ash. Lahars are very dangerous hazards.

Lateral erosion – The process by which a river can cut sideways into its own river bank. Lateral erosion means that, over time, meanders can cut across the floodplain of a river.

Less Economically Developed Countries (LEDC) – The countries that are to the south of the Brandt Line in Central and South America, Africa and parts of Asia. Most LEDCs have lower incomes than **More Economically Developed Countries (MEDCs)**.

Liquefaction – A soil process that can occur during a strong earthquake. Water in the soil is forced upwards by the shaking. The water pushes the soil particles apart, turning the ground to jelly. This process causes the sinking (or subsidence) of buildings.

Load – The sediment carried by a river.

M

Mantle – The part of the Earth that lies beneath the crust. The rocks in the mantle are hot and under pressure so they behave rather like plastic and deform easily. Some rocks in the mantle are molten.

Manufactured goods – Goods which have been produced in a factory or workshop.

Millennium Development Goals (MDGs) – These are targets set by the United Nations to try to encourage and measure improvements to human development.

Meander – A river landform. A sweeping curve or bend in the river's course.

Glossary

More Economically Developed Countries (MEDCs) – The countries that are to the north of the Brandt line in North America, Europe, northern Asia and parts of Oceania. Most MEDCs have higher incomes than **Less Economically Developed Countries (LEDCs)**.

Mouth – The point at which a river enters a lake or the sea.

N

Non-Government Organisations (NGOs) – Non-profit-making organisations, such as Oxfam, ActionAid or WaterAid, which are independent of the government.

O

Oceanic ridge – Long chains of mountains that run down the centre of several oceans, including down the middle of the Atlantic Ocean. The ocean ridges are formed by plate movement.

Oceanic trench – Long, deep gorges in the sea bed that occur around the edges of some oceans including the Pacific Ocean. The ocean trenches are formed by plate movement.

Overland flow – The flow of water across the ground surface.

P

Pastoral farmers – Farmers who keep grazing animals such as cattle or goats.

Peak discharge – The maximum flow of water recorded in a river during a flood event.

Percolate – A flow in the water cycle. The movement of water out of the soil and into the rocks below.

Photosynthesis – The processes that occurs in plants that uses the sun's energy to convert carbon dioxide to glucose.

Plate margin – The boundaries of the Earth's plates where they meet each other.

Plates – Rigid sections of crust. The plates lie on top of the mantle. They are able to move relative to each other. The movement is slow, but the force generated by their movement creates earthquakes and volcanic hazards.

Potholes – Rounded scour holes in the bedrock of a river or stream. Pot holes are formed when pebbles are turned in a circular motion by the flow of water.

Primary commodities – Raw materials which have not been processed, e.g. coal, minerals and unprocessed foodstuffs.

Primary hazards – Events which cause risk to human life during a volcanic eruption (such as pyroclastic flow) or earthquake (such as buildings collapsing due to ground shaking).

Primary health care – Primary health care is the first point of contact between a health care worker and a patient. It may involve preventative care, for example, immunisation.

Pyroclastic flow – A landslide of hot ash, rocks and gases from a violent volcanic eruption. Pyroclastic flows move at great speed. They usually contain gases that are several hundred degrees Celsius.

Q

Quality of life – A measure of the happiness and contentment of an individual or family.

R

Refugees – People who are in danger and who leave their homes for their own safety.

Renewable – Something useful to people that is capable of replacing itself. Water, forests and wind energy are all examples of renewable resources.

Rift valley – A steep sided valley formed by the pulling apart (or rifting) of the Earth's crust during plate movement.

S

Saltation – The process by which sand sized particles bounce along the river bed in the flow of water.

Sanitation – The safe disposal and treatment of sewage and waste water.

Secondary hazards – Events which cause risk to human life sometime after a volcanic eruption or earthquake. For example, the spread of disease after an earthquake is a secondary hazard.

Shield volcano – A large volcano that has gentle slopes. Some of the volcanoes in Iceland and Hawaii have this shape.

Socio-economic – A combination of social and economic factors.

Soft engineering – Alternative method of reducing floods by planting trees or allowing areas to flood naturally.

Solar furnace – A renewable technology that uses the sun's energy. Mirrors collect and concentrate the sun's light to heat water. The resulting steam is used to turn a turbine and generate electricity.

Solution – The process which dissolves minerals from rocks into water.

Glossary

Source – The place where a river starts to flow.

Strato-volcano – A large, steep sided volcano formed from layers of solidified lava and ash that have been built up by many different eruptions.

Subduction zone – The region on the earth's crust where one plate is destroyed as it is slowly pulled underneath another plate.

Subglacial – Any process or feature that occurs beneath a glacier or ice sheet. In Iceland there are a several powerful subglacial volcanoes that erupt under the ice.

Supervolcano – A volcano that erupts with the greatest possible force and produces the largest amounts of ash and other materials.

Suspension – The process of transport which carries fine sediment such as silt for long distances down a river.

Sustainable community – A community which is designed to have minimal impacts on the environment. Such communities may make use of energy efficiency, renewable technologies and also make use of local employment and services to reduce the impacts of commuting.

T

Tele-working – Jobs where most of the working week is spent working from home. Tele-working (or tele-cottaging) has been made more widely available by the use of personal computers, mobile technology and the internet.

Tephra – A term that describes all the fragments that are thrown from a volcano during an eruption. The hot rocks are full of gas when the volcano erupts so tephra often has a honeycomb texture (like pumice).

Throughflow – The downhill flow of water through soil.

Tiltmeter – A scientific instrument that is used to measure tilting of the ground. Tiltmeters can be used to measure small changes in ground shape that occur when the magma chamber beneath a volcano is filling with molten rock.

Traction – The process of transport which describes the movement of larger pebbles and cobbles as they roll along the bed of a river.

Trade bloc – Trading partnerships between different countries. The European Union is one example.

Transport – The movement of material through the landscape.

U

Urban heat island – When a city has temperatures that are warmer than in the surrounding rural area.

Urban micro-climate – The small-scale, local climate of a large city which is influenced by its buildings and traffic.

Urbanisation – The physical and human growth of towns and cities.

U-shaped valley – A trough shaped valley with very steep sides and a flat bottom that has been eroded by a glacier.

V

V-shaped valley – A valley with sides that slope sharply down to a river which has only the narrowest of floodplains. V-shaped valleys are formed where a river is actively cutting downwards into the landscape.

W

Water stress – When people do not have access to enough clean water.

Weather – Features such as temperature, rainfall, cloud cover, and wind as they are experienced. Measurements of these features can be recorded over long periods of time and averages calculated. These averages are what we call **climate**.

Index

Index